Withdrawn

DIANA HENRY

SIMPLE

effortless food, big flavors

MITCHELL BEAZLEY

An Hachette UK Company
www.hachette.co.uk

First published in Great Britain in 2016
by Mitchell Beazley, a division of
Octopus Publishing Group Ltd.
Carmelite House
50 Victoria Embankment
London EC4Y 0DZ
www.octopusbooks.co.uk
www.octopusbooksusa.com

Distributed in the US by Hachette Book Group
1290 Avenue of the Americas, 4th and 5th Floors
New York, NY 10020

Distributed in Canada by Canadian Manda Group
664 Annette St., Toronto, Ontario, Canada M6S 2C8

To Lucy, with love and thanks

ISBN 978 1 78472 204 3

Printed and bound in China

10 9 8 7 6 5 4 3 2 1

Publisher: Denise Bates
Art Director: Jonathan Christie
Photographer: Laura Edwards
Design and Art Direction: Miranda Harvey
Editor: Lucy Bannell
Home Economist and Food Stylist: Joss Herd
Assistant Home Economist: Rachel Wood
Senior Production Manager: Katherine Hockley

CRAZY   DIANA HENRY

contents

6

introduction

In 2004 I wrote a book called *Pure Simple Cooking*, full of the kind of dishes I began to make when my first child was born. He cried constantly, so I was always carrying him and had no hands free. The more elaborate cooking I'd enjoyed before his arrival went out the window. In fact I ate takeout pizzas for quite a few weeks after his birth, often through tears as I wondered how I would ever manage to cook again. Gradually, I started to make dishes that were just stuck in the oven. I didn't mind if they took a long time to cook, only about whether they took a long time to prepare. I couldn't do stir-fries—too much chopping—and rarely made risottos. It has meant a lot to me that people cite *Cook Simple* as a cookbook that really helped them. It's not because it is a book of quick food, but a book of *low-effort* food. Noncooks and unsure cooks use it as much as people who feel totally at home in the kitchen.

Now the baby that forced me to change my cooking style is 17. I still—certainly during the week—like to cook food that doesn't take much hands-on time, and still throw a lot of dishes in the oven. But my life has changed; I can now manage risottos midweek, also fish or meat cooked on a ridged grill pan and served with a relish, or cooked in a skillet in which a simple sauce is made. There are a few things—dals and other pulse dishes—which can simmer away on the stove while I do something else. So I felt it was time for a follow-up to *Cook Simple*; time to offer a new collection of simple dishes that use a wider range of techniques.

I still think in "blocks" when I wonder what to make for supper every day: fillets of fish—salmon or cod—or whole small fish, chops, sausages, pasta, chicken thighs, or potatoes for baking. I'm sure most people approach the evening meal like this. We buy what we can pick up easily on the way home, often from a small supermarket, or a local butcher or fish dealer. But this range of blocks has expanded. Our eating has changed in the last decade. Now I consider grains—often whole grains—pulses, and a lot more vegetables, too. They don't have to be "sides" to meat or fish, and this shift is reflected in the book.

UNUSUAL INGREDIENTS

The range of uncommon foodstuffs we eat—miso, pomegranate molasses, specific varieties of chiles—has also grown in the last decade. I don't use these just for the hell of it, but because I think they make eating more interesting, or are part of a cuisine I like. Most unusual items are now available online (and supermarkets have a vast array), but I've given alternatives where possible. There's a list of online suppliers at the back of the book, too. The matter of unfamiliar ingredients divides people: I get as many letters telling me they love discovering something new as I do from people complaining that they can't get pomegranate molasses at the corner store.

HOW MANY PEOPLE DO THE RECIPES SERVE?

This was one of the hardest things to decide when writing the recipes. People have different appetites and I think we all, generally, eat less than we used to. My partner will always eat two chicken thighs, for example, but my kids only ever have one each. So consider who you are serving and what their appetites are like. When it comes to grain, salad, and vegetable recipes, the question is even more difficult, since now we eat vegetable dishes as a main course. I've given as much guidance as I could. As a general rule, when it comes to vegetable dishes that serve six as a side dish, the recipe will serve four as a main meal.

COOKING EQUIPMENT

I never read those pages where writers lay out what you should have in your kitchen. For years—even after I started writing about food—I had the worst-equipped kitchen: not enough saucepans; one skillet; a limited range of knives. . . But, apart from basics, there are a few things that will make cooking from this book easier. I often use a 12-inch diameter, shallow broad cast-iron casserole with a lid. It's the most useful dish in my kitchen, and many of the recipes were tested in it, so the cooking times are right for this size and dimension of dish. It's brilliant for throw-it-in-the-oven dishes as it allows chicken and vegetables to lie in a single layer and roast, rather than sweat as they would if they were piled on top of one another.

Roasting pans of various sizes are useful. If I say a leg of lamb or a chicken has to fit "snugly" in a pan it's because the juices (especially when there's honey in a marinade) will burn if the space around the meat is too great. A gratin dish is important and a pudding basin or pie dish, too.

I also have a food processor and wouldn't be without it. Electric beaters—you don't need a food mixer—are good for batters and whipping cream and are not expensive. It seems a small thing, but for grating ginger and garlic—and they appear a lot in this book—I use a Cuisipro fine grater. They're not cheap but they save time and hassle and are the best on the market, in my opinion. Finally, a pestle and mortar. I realize that might seem a little old-fashioned, but there are a lot of dishes in this book that require a bit of bashing. I like texture and sometimes food processors chop things too finely, especially if your attention wavers for a moment. So, a shallow cast-iron casserole with a lid, a pie dish, a few roasting pans, a gratin dish, a pestle and mortar, a good grater, and—if you can—a food processor are all good to have.

There are two types of dish in *Simple*. Most are dishes you can cook midweek for your family, or for you and your partner; some are for weekend meals—Friday or Saturday night supper or Sunday lunch—to serve to friends (these are still simple, but take a bit more effort). There's no one who can't cook. You don't need many skills to feed yourself, your friends, and family well. If you can shove a tray of red bell peppers into the oven, or cook pasta until al dente, you can make great food. What we mostly lack are ideas. That's what I tried to give in *Cook Simple* and, again, here. You don't have to be a chef. I'm not. You just need some inspiration to help you turn the ordinary—the building blocks of meals—into something special.

EGGS

egg & salmon donburi

DONBURI ARE JAPANESE dishes. They are simple concoctions served
on a bowl of rice. I've stolen this particular donburi from the Japanese
restaurant Nobu and adapted it. At the restaurant they serve it on sushi
rice, but you can use basmati, or not bother with the rice at all. It sounds
quite Puritan, but is really rich and satisfying; very quick to make, too.
I sometimes have pickled ginger and a dab of wasabi with it.

SERVES 2

½ cup brown or white basmati rice

5½oz salmon fillet, skinned

2 teaspoons extra virgin olive oil

2 tablespoons minced onion

3 large eggs, lightly beaten

1 tablespoon sake or dry sherry

1 to 2 tablespoons light soy sauce

2 to 3 tablespoons finely chopped avocado tossed
   with a little lemon juice

sesame seeds, black or white

1 sheet of toasted nori (optional)

Cook the rice in boiling water while you make the rest of the dish. With brown rice, just cook it
until tender (about 25 minutes). If you're cooking white rice, add just enough water to cover by
about 1 inch. Bring to a boil and, when the rice looks "pitted" on the surface, reduce the heat to
its lowest, cover, and let cook for 10 to 12 minutes, then fork it through.

To cook the salmon, put about 2 inches of water in a pan and, when it's at a gentle simmer,
add the fish. Cover and poach over very low heat for about two minutes. You want it raw in the
middle but cooked around the outside (though cook it right through if you prefer). Keep it warm.

Heat the olive oil in a small skillet and gently sauté the onion until it is soft but not colored. Mix
the eggs with the sake or sherry, add to the pan, and cook very gently, stirring, until you have a
creamy mixture like soft scrambled eggs. Flake the warm fish and mix it with the soy sauce.

Divide the rice between two bowls. Top each with half the eggs, fish, avocado, and sesame seeds,
then crumble on the nori, if using. Add keta if you're going for luxury. Serve immediately.

persian-inspired eggs with dates & chili

I LOVE THE IRANIAN FOOD SHOP, Persepolis, in south London. The first time I visited, I ate this fabulous dish in the café there, cooked by the owner, Sally Butcher. I have changed the recipe a bit—added some greens and onion—to make it into a more substantial lunch (Sally serves it with flatbread for breakfast). It sounds like a strange combination, I know, but it's addictive.

SERVES 1

½ tablespoon olive oil
½ onion, finely sliced
½ teaspoon cumin seeds
¼ teaspoon chili flakes
handful of baby spinach
2 large eggs, lightly beaten
salt and pepper
2 soft dates (such as Medjool), pitted and coarsely chopped
1 tablespoon coarsely chopped cilantro leaves
Greek yogurt and flatbread, to serve (optional)

Heat the olive oil in a small skillet and add the onion. Cook over medium heat until it is golden and soft. Add the cumin and chili flakes and cook for another 30 seconds or so, then add the spinach. Keep turning the leaves over in the heat so they wilt and the moisture that comes out of them evaporates, then reduce the heat and add the eggs, seasoning, and dates.

Cook quite gently, just as you would if you were making creamy scrambled eggs; the mixture should be soft set. Finally scatter with the cilantro. Serve immediately, with a little yogurt on the side (if you've made quite a spicy plateful you'll need it) and flatbread, if you want.

menemen

I HAD ONLY EVER MADE menemen with baked eggs (the recipe
is in my book *Plenty*) until a vacation in Turkey a few years back
when, every day, I had this version. I could honestly have eaten it for
breakfast, lunch, and dinner. Never have scrambled eggs tasted so
good. Be careful to ensure that the vegetable mixture isn't too wet
when you add the eggs.

SERVES 3 TO 4

For the menemen
1 large leek
2 tablespoons olive oil
1 red bell pepper, seeded and finely chopped
1 green bell pepper, seeded and finely chopped
salt and pepper
2 garlic cloves, crushed
pinch of chili flakes, or ½ teaspoon cayenne pepper
4 tomatoes, seeded and chopped
5 large eggs, lightly beaten

To serve (all optional)
warm flatbread
chopped dill, cilantro, or parsley leaves
crumbled feta cheese
plain yogurt

Remove the coarse outer leaves of the leek and trim the top—you need to get rid of the more
tatty looking leaves—and the base. Slit the leek lengthwise and hold it under running water,
fanning out the leaves and washing it well to get rid of any trapped soil. Chop it.

Heat the olive oil in a large skillet. Add the leek, bell peppers, and seasoning and cook over
medium heat—reduce the heat if they start to color too much—until almost completely soft.
Add the garlic and chili flakes or cayenne and cook for a minute, then add the tomatoes (to seed
tomatoes, quarter them, then just scoop or cut out the seeds from the surrounding flesh). Cook
until they are soft, too, and their moisture has mostly evaporated (you might need to increase
the heat to do this). It's important that the mixture isn't too wet, or the eggs won't scramble well.

Season the eggs, add them to the pan, and cook over very low heat, stirring all the time, until
just set. Serve immediately with flatbread and any of the other accompaniments.

eggs with bell peppers & 'nduja

'NDUJA IS AN INGREDIENT that will become mainstream before too long. It's an intensely spicy pork paste from Calabria. You can get it in Italian delis and some online supermarkets now stock it, too.

SERVES 4
⅓ cup olive oil, divided
1 large onion, minced
3 red bell peppers, seeded and sliced
salt and pepper
14oz cooked potatoes (unpeeled if waxy, peeled if floury), cut into chunks
3oz 'nduja
2 tablespoons extra virgin olive oil
4 large eggs

Heat 3 tablespoons of the regular olive oil in a large skillet or sauté pan (preferably one you can serve from) and add the onion, bell peppers, and seasoning. Cook until the vegetables are soft—about 25 minutes—keeping an eye on them and stirring every so often.

Meanwhile, heat the remaining regular olive oil in another skillet and sauté the potatoes until they're golden and crusty all over. Season well.

Add the potatoes to the onion and bell peppers, toss together, and add the 'nduja. Stir to break up the 'nduja and mix it well with the vegetables.

Heat the extra virgin olive oil in the pan you used for the potatoes and fry the eggs until the yolks have just set. Put the eggs on top of the 'nduja mixture and serve.

huevos rotos

Spanish "broken eggs." Spicy, cheap, calls for a cold beer.
Perfect midweek food, in other words.

Serves 2

⅓ cup extra virgin olive oil

1 large onion, very finely sliced

14oz round red or round white potatoes, peeled or unpeeled, sliced

salt and pepper

2 garlic cloves, crushed

2½ teaspoons smoked paprika

¼ teaspoon chili flakes

2 to 4 eggs, depending on appetite

Heat the olive oil in a large nonstick skillet over medium heat and add the onion and potatoes. Fry for about 12 minutes, or until the potatoes are soft right through and everything is golden. Season, add the garlic and spices, and cook for another four minutes.

Break the eggs one by one into the pan. You need to do this from a height of at least 12 inches so that the eggs crash into the mixture. Season with salt and pepper and let them cook for a minute or so without stirring. You can scoop up some oil from the edge of the pan (tilt the pan so you can do this) and spoon it over the eggs to help them set. Pierce the eggs—they are *rotos*, after all—so the yolks are just starting to run before serving.

sure as eggs

EGGS ARE A MIRACLE of natural architecture: delicate, lovely to hold, and somehow complete in themselves. They've been enjoying something of a renaissance lately, partly due to the modern popularity of breakfast and brunch as a social occasion, but also because we find them so comforting. They're packed with protein, are perfect for vegetarians and those cutting down their meat intake, and have been given a clean bill of health, too. We now know that the dietary cholesterol in eggs doesn't have a significant effect on blood cholesterol. You can go to work on an egg and come home on one, too.

Time was when we couldn't think much beyond boiled and scrambled. Now I rustle up egg dishes from Japan, Iran, and Turkey and not just when there's nothing but eggs in the house. These are dishes I love. This chapter isn't about constructing risky soufflés, or sweating over glorious but demanding unguents. such as hollandaise. It's about getting lunch or supper on the table quickly and easily, but with a bit of pizzazz.

Eggs need to be cooked with care, though. The biggest mistake we make with them is to apply too fierce a heat. Hot is fine if you're frying an egg and want a frilly edge, but most of the time high heat just makes eggs rubbery. Scrambled eggs, in particular, need to be cooked low and slow (adding a walnut-size lump of butter at the end helps stop them from cooking any further). A panful of creamy, just-set scrambled eggs is one of the most luxurious things you can eat. Make the Japanese dish on page 10 and you'll see just how rich they can be. You shouldn't cook boiled eggs fiercely either, just at a vigorous simmer, otherwise the shells will crack. When poaching, use really fresh eggs—that stops the whites from splaying—and very gently simmering water. Crack your egg into a cup, then carefully slide it into the pan. (I find that poaching in a skillet works best.)

I care about the quality of the food I eat, and about its provenance, but I also try to be realistic about what people can afford. When it comes to flavor, though, there are some foods about which I cannot compromise: pork, butter, and eggs are the three I would prefer not to eat at all if I couldn't get the best, as I know I will be disappointed with them. For years I bought standard free-range eggs. Now I buy eggs from specific breeds—mostly Burford Browns and Cotswold Legbars (I can find them in supermarkets here in the UK, and don't have to go to directly to a farm)—because they taste so much better. If eggs are going to be the star of your lunch or supper, I think that the extra expense is more than justified (and compared to other foods, the extra is not *that* much). There's a bowl of pale blue Cotswold Legbar eggs on my kitchen counter right now. They aren't just beautiful, they also have limitless potential.

greens with chili, olive oil, eggs, feta & seeds

MUCH QUICKER TO MAKE than it first appears. Fry the eggs rather than poaching, if it's easier (it always is for me).

SERVES 2

3½oz kale, coarse stalks removed, leaves torn

3 tablespoons extra virgin olive oil, divided, plus a little more to serve

4½oz spinach, thick stalks removed, coarsely chopped

2 small garlic cloves, finely sliced

¼ teaspoon chili flakes

salt and pepper

2 tablespoons coarsely chopped parsley or cilantro leaves

squeeze of lemon juice

2 large eggs

2 slices of sourdough bread

2½ tablespoons crumbled feta cheese

2 teaspoons pumpkin seeds, or any other seeds you prefer

Put the kale into a pot of boiling water and blanch it for five minutes. Drain it really well, then squeeze out the water using your hands.

Heat 2 tablespoons of the extra virgin olive oil in a skillet and add the kale and spinach. Cook over medium–high heat until the kale is heated through, the spinach has wilted, and the water that comes out of the spinach has evaporated; this is *very* important. Add the remaining oil and the garlic and chili flakes. Sauté gently until the garlic is pale gold and everything is hot. Add the seasoning, herbs, and a squeeze of lemon juice (the mixture should be warm and glossy). Cover to keep warm.

Quickly poach the eggs (see page 19) and toast the bread. Drizzle with a little olive oil. Pile the greens onto the toast, top each serving with an egg, scatter with the feta cheese and seeds, and serve immediately.

leek & feta omelet with sumac

WE SHOULD MAKE MORE EFFORT with omelets. They tend to be
made when there are only eggs in the house and cooked over heat
this is too high, giving a rubbery result. Think about the filling; cook
it separately and let your imagination go. Try leek with goat cheese
and chopped black olives, or apple, leek, and smoked Cheddar. These
instructions are for one large omelet to serve two, but you can cook
two smaller omelets instead, if you prefer.

SERVES 2

1 large leek

½ tablespoon olive oil

salt and pepper

1 garlic clove, crushed

2 to 3 teaspoons unsalted butter

4 large eggs, lightly beaten

½ cup crumbled feta cheese

good pinch of sumac (optional)

Remove the coarse outer leaves of the leek and trim the tops—you need to get rid of the more
tatty looking leaves—and the base. Slit the leek lengthwise and hold it under running water,
fanning out the leaves and washing it well to get rid of any trapped soil. Cut into pieces 1¼ to
1½ inches long.

Heat the oil in a nonstick skillet, add the leek and seasoning, and cook over medium heat until
completely soft (but not colored; reduce the heat if it starts to brown). The mixture should be
quite dry, so if it's at all wet increase the heat to drive off excess moisture. Add the garlic and
cook for another couple of minutes. Check the seasoning, then scrape into a bowl.

Melt the butter in the same pan over medium–low heat. Season the eggs, then add them to
the pan. Using a wooden spoon, push the parts that are getting firm into the middle and swish
the uncooked eggs around until they set as well. The bottom should be just firm but the top
still a little runny.

Spoon the leeks and scatter the feta on half of the omelet, then, using a metal spatula, fold the
other half on top. Sprinkle with the sumac, if using (it just adds a tart citrus note), and serve.

parsi-style scrambled eggs

WHEN I'M DYING FOR A CURRY, I sometimes make this for supper; it sates that craving for a fraction of the price. The addition of a little cream makes it luxurious, too. Eat with warm naan bread.

SERVES 2

2 teaspoons unsalted butter

½ small onion, minced

½ to 1 red chile, depending on how hot you like it, seeded and finely chopped

1 garlic clove, minced

2 plum tomatoes, seeded and finely chopped

4 large eggs, lightly beaten

2 tablespoons heavy cream (optional)

salt and pepper

2 tablespoons finely chopped cilantro leaves

Melt the butter in a nonstick skillet over medium heat. Add the onion and cook, stirring from time to time, until soft but not colored. Add the chile and garlic and cook for a further two minutes, then add the tomatoes and cook until they have softened. Increase the heat to drive off excess moisture from the tomatoes, or the eggs won't scramble well.

Add the eggs, cream, if using, seasoning and half the cilantro, then cook over medium–low heat, stirring the eggs with a wooden spoon, until they form soft curds. Go slowly and gently. Scatter with the rest of the cilantro and serve immediately.

SALADS

grilled zucchini, burrata & fregola

Fregola is a Sardinian pasta, about the size and shape of hailstones. If you can't find it, you could use Israeli couscous—that's the chunky type—since it looks quite similar. You can also use mozzarella if you can't find burrata.

Serves 6 as a side dish, 4 as a main course
6 large or 12 medium zucchini
¼ cup olive oil, divided
salt and pepper
7oz fregola
2 tablespoons extra virgin olive oil, plus more to serve
7oz burrata cheese
1½oz pecorino cheese, shaved, plus more to serve
leaves from 1 big bunch of basil, plus more to serve
juice of 1 large lemon

Cut the zucchini diagonally into disks about ¼ inch in thickness. Heat some of the regular olive oil in a large skillet and cook the zucchini, in batches, until golden on each side and tender. With each batch you need to start on high heat to get a good color, then reduce the heat so the slices can cook through. Season as you go and use more oil as you need it. Transfer each batch of cooked zucchini to a dish.

Cook the fregola in boiling salted water for 15 minutes, or following the package directions, then drain, shake off the excess water, and put into a mixing bowl. Toss with the extra virgin olive oil and seasoning.

Tear the burrata cheese into chunks. Layer the various ingredients—zucchini, burrata cheese, pecorino cheese, basil, fregola, lemon juice, and more extra virgin olive oil—in a broad shallow serving bowl. Finish with basil, shavings of pecorino cheese, and a final drizzle of extra virgin olive oil. Serve while still warm, or at room temperature.

cucumber, radishes & cherries with rose petals

THIS IS LIKE EATING A GARDEN. It's fresh and pretty with both crisp and soft textures. Mint or dill work just as well as tarragon.

SERVES 4

For the dressing
¾ tablespoon white wine vinegar
smidgen of Dijon mustard
salt and pepper
⅓ cup olive oil
1½ tablespoons heavy cream
chopped leaves from 7 sprigs of tarragon
1½ teaspoons superfine sugar, or to taste

For the salad
1 small cucumber, or ½ large cucumber (about 9oz)
1½ cups cherries
5½oz radishes (ideally both crimson and purple), trimmed and shaved or very finely sliced
1½oz pea shoots
handful of unsprayed rose petals, torn if large, left whole if small

To make the dressing, mix the vinegar, mustard, and seasoning in a small bowl. Whisk in the oil and cream with 1½ tablespoons of water. Add the tarragon and sugar. Mix and taste; you may want to adjust the seasoning. The consistency should be about that of light cream.

Peel the cucumber in stripes, so some of the skin is left on (it just looks nice). Halve lengthwise and scoop out the seeds with a teaspoon. Discard them. Cut into slices about ⅛ inch thick, or cut the cucumber into ribbons using a vegetable peeler.

Pit the cherries; I like to tear them in half to do this, rather than cut them. Put the cucumber, radishes, and pea shoots into a broad shallow serving bowl and toss together with three-quarters of the dressing. Add the cherries and drizzle with the remaining dressing (the cherry juice "bleeds" over the salad, so it's best to add them last). Scatter with the rose petals and serve.

cumin-coriander roast carrots with pomegranates & avocado

AN IDEA SHAMELESSLY STOLEN from New York-based chef April Bloomfield and slightly fiddled around with. Roasted carrots and avocados are surprisingly good together. This makes a very grand platter to open a meal, or serve it on the side with roast chicken, or with another vegetable dish.

SERVES 6 as an appetizer, or 8 as a side dish

For the salad
30 young carrots, ideally slim
¼ cup extra virgin olive oil
2 teaspoons cumin seeds
1½ teaspoons coriander seeds, crushed
1 teaspoon chili flakes
salt and pepper
3 ripe avocados
3½ tablespoons walnut pieces, toasted (page 112)
3½oz watercress, coarse stalks removed
leaves from a small bunch of cilantro

1 cup Greek yogurt
1 garlic clove, crushed
seeds from ½ pomegranate

For the dressing
1 tablespoon pomegranate molasses
1 garlic clove, crushed
¼ teaspoon Dijon mustard
⅓ cup extra virgin olive oil
¼ teaspoon honey
squeeze of lemon juice

Preheat the oven to 400°F. Trim the carrots at the top but leave a little of green tuft on. If you can't find slim carrots, halve or quarter large ones. Don't peel them; just wash them well. Put in a roasting pan in which they can lie in a single layer. Add the olive oil, spices, and seasoning. Turn the carrots over in this to ensure they are all well coated. Roast in the oven for about 30 minutes; they will become tender and shrink slightly. Be careful not to overcook them.

To make the dressing, just beat everything together with a fork. Halve and pit the avocados, cut into slices, then carefully peel each slice. Put everything except the yogurt, garlic, and pomegranates into a broad shallow bowl (or onto a platter) and gently toss in three-quarters of the dressing. Mix the yogurt with the garlic and dot spoonfuls of this among the vegetables, then scatter with the pomegranate seeds. Spoon on the rest of the dressing and serve.

tomatoes, soft herbs & feta with pomegranate

A SALAD I FIRST ATE IN ISTANBUL. The pomegranate flavor here is in the dressing, not in the seeds. You can make this salad even when pomegranates are not in season.

SERVES 6

For the dressing
1 tablespoon white balsamic vinegar
1 tablespoon pomegranate molasses
1 teaspoon honey
1 garlic clove, crushed
salt and pepper
3 tablespoons extra virgin olive oil
lemon juice, to taste (optional)

For the salad
handful of flat-leaf parsley leaves
1lb 2oz well flavored tomatoes (a mixture of colors
    is lovely if you can find them)
handful of dill fronds, coarsely torn
2 small shallots, very finely sliced
5½oz barrel-aged feta cheese, drained of brine
¼ cup pomegranate seeds (optional)

Put the vinegar, pomegranate molasses, honey, garlic, and seasoning into a small bowl, then whisk in the olive oil. Taste for seasoning. Add a squeeze of lemon juice if you think it needs it.

Set aside some of the best-shaped parsley leaves and coarsely chop the rest.

Slice the tomatoes, or halve them if they are small. Put into a serving dish and add the dill, chopped parsley, shallots, and dressing. Crumble the feta cheese on top.

Toss very gently—you don't want to break up the feta cheese too much—then scatter with the pomegranate seeds, if using, and the whole parsley leaves. Serve immediately.

root, shiitake & noodle salad with miso dressing

I LOVE BROWN RICE NOODLES. They're so earthy. If you want to extend this, add shredded sugar snap peas (sliced lengthwise, no need to cook), edamame, finely sliced radishes, even avocado. This dressing is great. It's worth making double or even triple the amount here and keeping it in the fridge. It will soon disappear.

SERVES 8 as a side dish, 4 as a main course

For the dressing
4 teaspoons white miso
1 tablespoon honey
2 teaspoons rice vinegar
1 red chile, seeded and finely sliced
3 tablespoons peanut oil
2 teaspoons soy sauce
2 teaspoons sesame oil
3 tablespoons sweet pickled ginger, finely chopped

For the salad
3½oz mooli (daikon), cut into matchsticks
2 medium carrots, peeled
2 tablespoons peanut oil
14oz shiitake mushrooms, sliced
salt and pepper
8oz brown rice noodles
4¼oz baby spinach
6 scallions, trimmed and chopped at an angle
2 teaspoons white sesame seeds
2 teaspoons black sesame seeds (or more white sesame)

To make the dressing, whisk the miso, honey, and vinegar together, then whisk in everything else. It will seem quite strong, but you're going to add it to noodles so it needs to be assertive. Drop the mooli matchsticks into iced water to crisp up. Cut the carrots into matchsticks, or shave them: trim the tops, set them on the work top, and peel them, working away from yourself. When one side is flat, turn it and do the other side. You'll have some left, so keep it for something else.

Heat the oil in a skillet and briskly cook the mushrooms over high heat. Season well.

Put the noodles into boiling water and let soak for eight minutes. Drain and rinse in cold water. Shake excess water out, then throw into a serving bowl with half the dressing; I find it easiest to toss this with my hands. Drain the mooli; add to the bowl with the carrots, mushrooms, spinach, and scallions. Drizzle with the remaining dressing, sprinkle with the sesame seeds, and serve.

cool greens with hot asian dressing

You can put whatever you like in this as long as it's green—kale, Chinese leaf, small zucchini, raw young peas, fava beans, whatever. You can reduce the range, too, so you don't have to use all the herbs. Take care with the dressing. It needs a good sweet-sour-salty-hot balance, so taste and adjust it as you go before tossing with the vegetables.

SERVES 6 TO 8

For the dressing

1½ generous tablespoons superfine sugar, or to taste

juice of 2 to 3 limes (they vary a lot in juiciness), or to taste

1½ tablespoons fish sauce, or to taste

¾-inch piece ginger root, peeled and finely grated

2 red chiles, seeded and very finely chopped

1 garlic clove, crushed

¾ tablespoon sunflower or peanut oil

For the greens

½ cup edamame beans

1 avocado

juice of 1 lime

salt and pepper

3½oz sugar snap peas, sliced lengthwise

2¾oz mooli (daikon), cut into matchsticks, or radishes, finely sliced

½ cucumber, peeled and chopped

3 scallions, trimmed and chopped

1¾oz baby spinach, or mixed green salad leaves

leaves from 1 bunch each of cilantro, basil, and mint

sesame seeds, ideally mixed black and white

Using a fork, whisk the sugar with 1½ tablespoons of boiling water to help the sugar dissolve. Add the lime juice (reserve a little, as limes vary in juiciness). Add the fish sauce, ginger, chiles, and garlic, then beat in the oil. Taste for sweet-salty balance. You might want more lime juice, or even more sugar or fish sauce. Use your taste buds, but remember this is a strong dressing.

Boil the edamame beans for three minutes, drain, and let cool. Halve the avocado, pit it, then slice. Peel each slice, squeeze lime juice over, and season. Put all the vegetables, leaves, and herbs into a broad shallow bowl. Toss with the dressing, scatter with the sesame seeds, and serve.

food52 team salad

FOOD52 IS ONE OF THE BEST food websites. Based in New York, it's
classy and well designed and has great recipes. I visit the site pretty
much every day, so it was a big thrill to meet the team behind it when
I was last in the States. This is the salad they rustled up for lunch
(I've tweaked it only a little), served with various cheeses and breads.
I had never felt well disposed toward kohlrabi, but this changed my mind.
If you can't find watermelon radish, just use more kohlrabi or beets.

SERVES 4 TO 6 as a side dish

4¼oz kohlrabi

½lb mixed beets (ideally regular, golden, and candy cane)

4¾oz watermelon radish

1 eating apple

2 tablespoons lemon juice

1 tablespoon white balsamic vinegar

1 teaspoon honey

salt and pepper

¼ cup extra virgin olive oil (a fruity rather than a bitter, grassy type)

2 tablespoons lightly toasted hazelnuts, halved (see page 281)

Peel the kohlrabi, beets, and watermelon radish. Shave them all on a mandoline, or cut very, very finely with a sharp knife. Do the same with the apple, leaving it whole and working from each side toward the core. That way you will get good circles, but without the core (just eat the flesh around that, cook's treat).

Make a dressing by mixing the lemon juice, vinegar, honey, and seasoning. Whisk in the oil.

Spread the vegetables and apple out in a broad shallow bowl, dressing them as you go, then scatter with the nuts. The crimson in the beets will start to stain everything else, so it's better to layer the vegetables than it is to toss them. Serve immediately.

salad of chorizo, avocado & bell peppers with sherry dressing

To make a more gutsy dish, balance a fried egg for each person on top before you scatter it with the bread crumbs.

Serves 4 as a main course

For the salad
3 red bell peppers, halved and seeded
olive oil
salt and pepper
2 ripe avocados
lemon juice
2oz open-crumbed loaf (sourdough or ciabatta),
    torn into small pieces
extra virgin olive oil
finely grated zest of ½ unwaxed lemon

8oz chorizo
14oz can of chickpeas, drained and rinsed
2¾oz arugula, baby spinach, lamb's lettuce, or
    watercress, coarse stalks removed
generous handful of cilantro leaves

For the dressing
1 tablespoon sherry vinegar
⅓ cup extra virgin olive oil
2 teaspoons medium sherry
1 teaspoon honey

Preheat the oven to 375°F. Drizzle the bell peppers with the regular olive oil, season, and roast for about 35 minutes, or until completely soft. Let cool a little.

Make the dressing by whisking everything together and seasoning well. Halve the avocados, pit them, and cut the flesh into slices lengthwise. Carefully peel each slice. Squeeze a little lemon juice over the avocados to keep them from discoloring, and season.

Slice the bell peppers (I don't remove the skins). Fry the torn-up bread in a little extra virgin olive oil over medium heat, tossing so it doesn't burn but becomes golden and crunchy. In the final stages of cooking, add the lemon zest and season. Remove and discard the chorizo skin and cut the meat into disks. Put 1 tablespoon of regular olive oil in a skillet and quickly sauté it on both sides until golden.

Gently toss everything, except the bread, with the dressing. Scatter with the bread and serve.

southeast asian fruit salad with chile & tamarind

BASED ON A SALAD called *rojak* or *rujak* (the word means "mixture" or "wild mix"). There are many variations, but some are almost entirely based on fruit. You could add matchsticks of raw jicama to this if you can find some, but I rarely can. The dressing usually contains shrimp paste, which I hate, so I've used fish sauce instead; use shrimp paste if you don't mind it. You can add herbs—cilantro, basil, or mint leaves, or a mixture—as well, even though that's not authentic.

SERVES 6 as a side dish

For the salad
1 Granny Smith apple
juice of 1 lime
2 mangoes, slightly under-ripe
2 cups fresh pineapple chunks
½ cucumber, peeled, cut into chunks
1⅓ cups cherry tomatoes, quartered
½ tablespoon sesame seeds
1½ tablespoons roasted peanuts,
    coarsely chopped

For the dressing
1 tablespoon tamarind paste
¾ tablespoon fish sauce
juice of ½ lime
1 tablespoon palm sugar, or soft light brown sugar
½ teaspoon sambal oelek (Indonesian chile paste),
    or to taste

Halve, core, and cut the apple into matchsticks, immediately dropping them into a serving dish with the lime juice (this stops it from discoloring). Peel the mangoes, then remove the "cheeks" (the rounded parts on each side). Cut into cubes, then remove the rest of the flesh as neatly as possible and cut that into cubes, too. Toss into the bowl with the pineapple, cucumber, and tomatoes.

For the dressing, stir the tamarind, fish sauce, and lime juice with the jaggery until it dissolves. Add the sambal oelek and 2 tablespoons of water. It will taste strong, but it works with the fruit.

Toss the dressing with the salad in the bowl and scatter with the sesame seeds and peanuts.

smoked trout, eggs & keta with sour cream dressing

A BEAUTIFUL LOOKING DISH that takes very little effort. Using keta (salmon caviar) does make it pricey, but I love those little bursts of saltiness against the potatoes and eggs. It's not an everyday ingredient, but it makes a lovely weekend lunch or brunch, and is just as good at Christmas as in spring.

SERVES 6 as a main course

For the salad
1lb 2oz baby potatoes
2 tablespoons white wine vinegar
½ cup fruity extra virgin olive oil, divided
salt and pepper
6 eggs
13oz smoked trout
2¼oz baby salad leaves (whatever you can find)
fronds from about 12 sprigs of dill, torn
¼oz chives, halved
¾oz jar of keta (salmon roe)

For the dressing
½ cup sour cream
1 tablespoon heavy cream
2 teaspoons Dijon mustard
juice of ½ small lemon

Boil or steam the potatoes until just tender. Slice them and gently mix in a bowl with the vinegar, two-thirds of the olive oil, and some seasoning. Let cool. Make the dressing by mixing everything together. Cook the eggs for seven minutes, run cold water over them to cool them a little, then peel and halve.

Flake the trout and gently combine in a bowl with the rest of the olive oil, seasoning, the potatoes (with their dressing), leaves, and herbs. Arrange on a platter—or in in a broad shallow bowl—and add the eggs. Spoon the creamy dressing over the top (or serve it under the salad) and dot with little spoonfuls of the keta. Serve immediately.

melon, blueberry & feta salad with ginger & mint

YES, I DO ADORE salads made with fruit, but melons can be musky and muted and blueberries—if you get good fruit—have a little tartness, too. Then there's the salty feta cheese to cut the sweetness. You can omit the blueberries here, if they seem a fruit too far.

SERVES 6 as a side dish, 4 as a main course

For the salad
6oz watermelon flesh, neatly sliced (seeds flicked out)
8½oz Ogen melon flesh (about ½ melon), neatly sliced
8½oz Galia melon flesh (about ½ melon), neatly sliced
½ cucumber, peeled
⅔ cup blueberries
¾oz mint leaves
1 cup crumbled or chopped barrel-aged feta cheese
1 tablespoon coarsely chopped pistachio nuts

For the dressing
juice of 2½ limes
3½ tablespoons vinegar from a jar of pickled ginger
1 tablespoon liquid honey
3½ tablespoons extra virgin olive oil
1 teaspoon peeled and finely grated ginger root
salt and pepper

Put the mixed melon flesh into a broad, shallow serving dish. Slice the cucumber very thinly and add it to the melon with the blueberries.

Mix everything for the dressing together.

Tear any large mint leaves in half, leaving small leaves whole, and add to the salad with most of the dressing. Scatter with the feta cheese and nuts, drizzle with the rest of the dressing, and serve.

warm salad of squid, bacon, beans & tarragon

IF YOU BUY CLEANED SQUID—and that's easy to get now—this is very quick to put together. It makes a good appetizer, light lunch, or supper. Add warm sliced round red or round white potatoes if you want to make it more substantial.

SERVES 3 TO 4

For the dressing
2 tablespoons lemon juice, plus more for the squid
2 tablespoons extra virgin olive oil
1/3 cup heavy cream
leaves from 6 sprigs of tarragon, chopped
salt and pepper

For the salad
1lb 5oz squid (preferably small), cleaned
½ tablespoon olive oil, divided, plus more for the squid
2 shallots, finely sliced
7oz bacon lardons
½lb French green beans, topped but not tailed

For the dressing, mix the lemon juice, extra virgin olive oil, cream, tarragon, and 2 tablespoons of water in a small bowl. Season.

Cut the wings from the squid and put them aside with the tentacles. Cut the bodies down one side so they open out. If your squid are big, halve the body lengthwise. Wash and dry the squid well using paper towels, then add to a bowl with enough regular olive oil to moisten them.

Gently cook the shallots in the ½ tablespoon of regular olive oil until they have lost their rawness but aren't soft. Put into a broad shallow serving bowl. Add the bacon to the same pan and cook over high heat until golden all over and cooked through. Add to the shallots. Cook the green beans in boiling water until al dente. Drain and run cold water over them. Pat dry and toss into the bowl.

Heat a skillet until very hot. Season the squid and cook it quickly on both sides in batches; you want to get a lovely golden color. Squeeze over lemon juice as soon as it's ready. Toss it with the other ingredients in the serving bowl. Spoon on the dressing and check the seasoning.

burrata with citrus, fennel & olives

QUITE A SPECIAL DISH—burrata isn't cheap—so this is more of a
treat recipe, though good mozzarella can be used instead of burrata.

SERVES 6

For the dressing
⅓ cup orange juice, or to taste
1 tablespoon lemon juice
2 teaspoons liquid honey, or to taste
⅓ cup extra virgin olive oil (fruity rather
than grassy), plus more for the burrata
salt and pepper

For the salad
2 oranges
1 pink grapefruit
1 white grapefruit
1 large fennel bulb
about 30 top-quality black olives, pitted
2 x 7oz burrata cheeses

Make the dressing by putting all the ingredients for it in a cup and whisking together with a
fork. Taste for seasoning and balance.

Cut a slice from the bottom and top of each citrus fruit so they have a flat base on which to sit.
Using a very sharp knife, cut the rind and the pith off, removing them in strips from top to
bottom and working your way around the fruit. Now slice the fruits, removing any seeds you see.

Quarter the fennel and remove the coarse outer leaves. Trim off any fronds and keep them for
later. Remove the core from each quarter, but don't allow the quarters to fall apart. Cut very
finely—wafer-thin slices are best—using a mandoline if you have one, or a very sharp knife.

Carefully toss the fennel, citrus, and olives together, or arrange them on plates, with the
dressing. Drain the burrata cheeses (be careful; they are fragile), then tear into pieces and put on
top of the salad, or serve them whole. Drizzle with extra virgin olive oil and sprinkle with some
freshly ground black pepper, if you like. Serve immediately.

no-hassle appetizers

Appetizers are my favorite part of any meal. They're small and light and they set the tone. I find it difficult not to offer an appetizer, even if I have friends around for supper midweek, so I've amassed a repertoire of dishes that take hardly any effort. Here are some of them.

QUICK-CURED SALMON & BUTTERMILK

This is stolen from the wonderful Stephen Harris at The Sportsman, in Kent, southeast England. Take 1lb 2oz good skinless salmon fillet, sprinkle with 7oz sea salt flakes mixed with 1 cup unpacked soft brown sugar. Cover and chill for 24 hours. Rinse and slice as you would smoked salmon. Mix 2½ tablespoons confectioner's sugar, the juice of 2 lemons, and ½ cup vodka. Marinate the salmon in this for 10 minutes. Mix 1 cup buttermilk, ½ teaspoon Dijon mustard, 1 tablespoon extra virgin olive oil, salt, and a pinch of sugar. Serve with the fish, shaved radishes, and dill.

DEVILED EGGS

The first thing I cooked in home economics class, these have had a renaissance. Boil 4 large eggs for 7 minutes. Let cool. Peel, halve, scoop out the yolks, and mash with 3 tablespoons good mayo, a walnut-size lump of soft butter, a good shake of Tabasco, 1 teaspoon chopped parsley, 1 teaspoon English mustard powder, and ½ teaspoon white wine vinegar. Season. Spoon this back into the whites, sprinkle with cayenne, and serve with all the sass of a Southern hostess.

ROASTED SPICED CHICKPEAS

I love potato chips but not with drinks (no matter how "posh"). For this good, easy alternative, preheat the oven to 375°F. Drain, rinse, and dry a 14-ounce can of chickpeas (or even 2, as people eat a lot once they start these). Toss them with 1 tablespoon olive oil, ½ tablespoon ground cumin, ½ tablespoon chili powder, salt, and pepper. Spread the chickpeas out on a baking pan and bake for 30 minutes, shaking the pan around every so often.

A LITTLE SCANDI FEAST

You don't even need to cook for this (except for the eggs). Serve cured herrings, a jar of keta, a bowl of sour cream with chopped dill, smoked fish, cured ham, sweet-savory pickled cucumber, cooked beets, and hard-boiled eggs. Offer rye bread or knäckebröd (you can get such good crispbreads these days), great butter, and chilled vodka. Good for brunch as well as for an appetizer.

CROSTINI WITH LARDO & HONEY

Seems just too easy? People will love it. Lightly toast slices of ciabatta; put furls of lardo on top; drizzle with good honey. That's it.

PEACHES WITH BURRATA

A perfect summer appetizer. Slice ripe peaches, carefully tear burrata, and put on a platter. Add basil, season, squeeze over lemon juice, and drizzle with your favorite olive oil. Tomatoes and Parma ham are optional additions.

SMOKED FISH BUTERBRODY

A Russian treat. Mash 10½oz good smoked trout or mackerel with 1½ tablespoons creamed horseradish, ⅓ cup soft butter, 1 tablespoon heavy cream, the yolks of 2 hard-boiled eggs, the juice of ½ lemon, salt, and pepper. Spread on squares of pumpernickel or rye (crusts off, and toasted if you're using rye).

PEAS & MELTED BUTTER

Yes, seriously. When they're young and have just come into season, boil them in their pods and serve in a bowl with a pot of melted butter.

MINIMAL MEZZE

This doesn't have to be a massive spread. Offer hot Moroccan or Middle Eastern pickles, really good taramasalata (not the dyed stuff), feta that you've marinated in extra virgin olive oil with some garlic, thyme, and chili flakes, roasted bell peppers (buy them in jars), olives, and flatbread. If you can manage something the day before, make labneh: put Greek yogurt into some fresh cheesecloth, form it into a bag, squeeze it, then set in a sieve over a bowl. Let the whey drip off in the fridge overnight. Drizzle with good extra virgin olive oil, and dust with za'atar, dukkah, or sumac.

PEA & 'NDUJA TOASTS

'Nduja is the chorizo *de nos jours*, a totally addictive spicy Calabrian pork paste that is catching on everywhere. Serve it on little toasted croûtes (ciabatta or slices of French bread). Purée ⅔ cup cooked peas with ½ crushed garlic clove, ½ tablespoon lemon juice, a few fresh mint leaves, 2 tablespoons extra virgin olive oil, ½ tablespoon heavy cream, and seasoning. Spoon onto the croûtes, then place chunks of 'njuda on top to serve.

TOAST

carrot hummus, roast tomatoes & harissa yogurt

THIS MAKES MORE HUMMUS than you need for a meal, but it's a real pain to use only half a can of anything. Keep the rest of the hummus in the fridge, where it will last for about three days. The tomatoes are really useful to have in the fridge, too. I often cook double quantities of them; they're great on toast with labneh (see page 51), eggs, or mashed avocado.

SERVES 4

For the roast tomatoes
8 plum tomatoes
2 tablespoons olive oil
½ tablespoon balsamic vinegar
2 teaspoons harissa
salt and pepper
1 teaspoon soft light brown sugar

For the hummus and yogurt
9oz carrots, peeled and chopped
14oz can of chickpeas, drained and rinsed
1 cup extra virgin olive oil
3½ tablespoons tahini
juice of 1½ lemons
½ teaspoon cayenne pepper
1 teaspoon ground cumin
1 cup Greek yogurt
1 tablespoon harissa
4 slices of sourdough bread, or bread of your choice

Preheat the oven to 375°F. Halve the tomatoes lengthwise and put in a small roasting pan or ovenproof dish; they need to fit fairly snugly in a single layer. Mix together the regular olive oil, vinegar, harissa, and some seasoning and pour this over the tomatoes. Turn the tomatoes over to coat them in the oil mixture, then rearrange them cut-side up. Sprinkle with the sugar and roast for 40 to 45 minutes, or until shrunken and sweet.

Cook the carrots in boiling water until they're tender. Drain, reserving some cooking liquid, then whizz in a food processor with everything else except the yogurt, harissa, and bread. Add some of the cooking water if needed to make the purée a little thinner. Scrape into a bowl.

Stir the yogurt to loosen it, put it into a bowl, and spoon on the harissa. Toast the bread and serve it with the hummus, tomatoes, and yogurt.

mumbai toastie

OH, MY. MY FRIEND ROOPA GULATI told me about these—they're
sold as street food in Mumbai—and I was a little skeptical about cheese
with spices, but these toasties now make a regular appearance in my
house. They're perfect for those nights when you're craving Indian food,
but don't want to spend money on a takeout, and it's a great supper to
eat while watching television. You'll want a cold beer.

SERVES 1

For the fresh chutney
½ green chile, seeded and chopped
handful of cilantro leaves
leaves from 8 sprigs of mint, torn
1 garlic clove, crushed
sea salt flakes
½ teaspoon superfine sugar
juice of ½ lemon

For the sandwich
2 slices of white bread
½ cup grated Cheddar cheese,
    or 1¾oz very finely sliced
1 tomato, sliced
¼ small red onion, very finely sliced
pinch of ground cumin
pinch of ground coriander
pinch of ground ginger
pinch of ground cinnamon
unsalted butter
1 teaspoon vegetable oil (optional)

Put everything for the chutney, except the lemon juice, in a mortar and pound it with the pestle.
You can just chop everything together instead, but the chutney is better if it has had a good
pounding. Add the lemon juice.

Spread the chutney onto both slices of the bread. Lay the cheese, tomato, and onion on one of
them and sprinkle with the spices. Set the other slice of bread on top.

If you have a sandwich grill, use it, buttering the outside of the sandwich as usual, or melt a
walnut-size lump of butter and the oil in a skillet and cook it over medium heat for about
3 minutes on each side, weighing it down (I use a flat saucepan lid with a heavy can on top).
Be careful not to burn the sandwich, and adjust the heat accordingly. The cheese should melt.
Serve immediately.

toast with crab & cilantro-chile mayo

A TREAT FOR TWO. Good for lunch on a Saturday.

SERVES 2

2 tablespoons mayonnaise

½ tablespoon heavy cream

finely grated zest of ½ lime, plus a couple of squeezes of lime juice

1 small red chile

2 tablespoons finely chopped cilantro leaves

2 slices of sourdough bread

salt and pepper

3½oz white crab meat, picked over

unsalted butter

2 small handfuls of watercress, coarse stalks removed

Mix the mayonnaise with the cream and add the lime zest and a squeeze of juice. Halve the chile, remove the seeds, and cut into fine shreds. Stir this and the cilantro into the mayonnaise and mix well.

Toast the sourdough, season the crab meat, and add another squeeze of lime juice. Butter the toast, put the crab on top, then add a good dollop of the mayo. (You can stir the mayonnaise into the crab and eat it that way, too, but I prefer to come across some plain, unadorned crab every now and again here.) Serve with watercress.

hard cider rarebit

ADDING AN EGG is not to everyone's taste (or everyone's idea of
what a rarebit should be), but I like it. It turns a snack into a very
good supper. And that's not the only twiddle you can make. Try this
with sautéed slices of apple or pear (lay these on the bread before
adding the cheese mixture); I've even been known to add bacon.
A green salad and a glass of hard cider are perfect on the side.

SERVES 2

2 tablespoons unsalted butter

2½ tablespoons all-purpose flour

½ cup hard dry cider

1 cup grated sharp Cheddar cheese

1 teaspoon English mustard (made mustard, not powder)

shake of Worcestershire sauce (optional)

2 slices of bread from a good crusty white loaf

pepper

1 egg, lightly beaten

½ tablespoon apple brandy or Calvados

Preheat the broiler: some can take quite a while to get hot enough.

Melt the butter in a saucepan and add the flour. Stir over medium heat until they blend and
thicken to form a roux. Take the pan off the heat and pour in the hard cider, a little at a time,
stirring well after each addition and beating to make sure no lumps form. Put the pan back on
the stove and stir as you bring the mixture to a boil. You should end up with a smooth, thick
sauce. Reduce the heat to low and add the cheese, mustard, and Worcestershire sauce, if using.

Toast the bread.

Stir the sauce to help the cheese melt completely, then remove from the heat, season with
pepper, and add the egg and brandy, stirring well. Divide between the two slices of toast
and broil until bubbling and golden.

crunch time

TOAST IS ESSENTIALLY a private pleasure, not something we often serve to others (except at breakfast). It's also, for me, the go-to emotional food. If I'm unhappy, I think I deserve toast. When I feel tired and need a pick-me-up, I wait for a slice of sourdough to pop. When I had post-natal depression, toast with lots of butter was the only food that could over-ride my lack of appetite and break through the bleakness. That makes it special. I'm not alone in my ardor. Toast is a British love. Chewy, warm, and slightly nutty, it's the mother of all comfort foods, a friend in good times and in bad.

Now that we take bread more seriously, we are beginning to think toast more important, too. As long as you use good bread and top it with something that has the healthy seal of approval (nut butter, crushed avocado, local honey), it's mandatory to show off your toast via Instagram and Twitter. When I met Apollonia Poilâne, whose family produce the world-famous Poilâne sourdough, she served me a feast of toast, explaining that sourdough actually tastes best several days after baking, toasted, as this brings out its characteristic tang. A few years back, San Franciscans—as is their wont—went all hipster about toast. Critics touted the $3 slice of artisanal toast as proof that this food-obsessed city had become a parody of itself. But they were doing good things with it. Cafés developed "toast bar" menus, and every time I visited a classy American food website someone had come up with a new twist on avo toast.

We Brits can claim a greater toast history than Californians, though. We've been putting interesting things on toast since the Middle Ages ("pokerounce," toast topped with hot honey, ginger, and cinnamon, sounds particularly good, as does quince purée with flower water). Then there are "savouries', specifically English treats of toast topped with anchovies, grated cheese, or ham and served at the end of dinner, so beloved of the Victorians and Edwardians. Food historian Dr. Annie Gray says we love toast because we have such a big bread culture in Britain. "Toast is a sensible way of using the remains of the loaf from the day before: it's thrifty. The kind of bread we like here lasts quite well, too, unlike French baguette, which is basically so hard the day after it's made, it's impossible to do anything with it."

Now toast has become the basis for a decent meal again: a proper lunch, a nourishing supper. It's especially useful if you're on your own, or there are just two of you. There are no rules about preparing it, though you should use good bread. Cheap sliced bread produced in a factory will be pappy inside; you want a toasted exterior and a good fluffy interior. It's also best to stand your newly toasted slice up against something so it cools just slightly before adding your topping. This prevents sogginess. And you wouldn't want that.

toasted brioche with boozy mushrooms

A REAL JOY. If you don't want the sweetness of brioche here, use toasted sourdough bread instead. This can take a fried egg on top, too. The obvious thing might be to add garlic and parsley but, in fact, unadulterated mushroominess is what you want.

SERVES 2

¼ to ½oz dried wild mushrooms

1½ tablespoons olive oil

9oz cremino mushrooms, or mixed mushrooms, coarsely chopped
   (you want quite big pieces)

2½fl oz dry sherry or vermouth

salt and pepper

⅓ cup heavy cream

2 slices of brioche loaf

Put the dried mushrooms in a small bowl and add enough boiling water to just cover them. Let stand for about 20 minutes.

Heat the oil in a skillet and add the fresh mushrooms. You'll think it's a lot for two people, but mushrooms really shrink. Cook them briskly over fairly high heat to get a good color. You need to keep moving them around. When they're golden brown and the juices they give off have evaporated, add the dried mushrooms with their soaking liquid. Cook until the soaking liquid has almost disappeared, then add the alcohol and seasoning. Cook over high heat until half the booze has disappeared, then add the cream.

Toast the brioche. Keep cooking the mushrooms until they are just coated in cream. Check for seasoning, then tip onto the toast and serve.

spiced avocado with black beans, sour cream & cheese

AVOCADO ON TOAST has almost become a cliché—I've lost count of the ways I've seen it prepared—but it's also irresistible (and good for you). This makes a little more of the avo-on-toast theme. Remember that the key to any avo toast is good seasoning.

SERVES 4

For the black beans
1 tablespoon olive oil
½ onion, minced
1 red bell pepper, seeded and chopped
   into small squares
2 garlic cloves, crushed
½ teaspoon ground cumin
⅓ cup chicken or vegetable stock
1 tablespoon orange juice
salt and pepper
14oz can of black beans, drained and rinsed
juice of ½ lime

For the toast
4 slices of sourdough bread
1 garlic clove
¼ cup extra virgin olive oil
4 small, ripe avocados
juice of 1 to 2 limes (depending on how juicy they are)
2 red chiles, seeded and finely sliced
4 scallions, finely chopped
¼ cup sour cream
2 tablespoons coarsely chopped cilantro leaves
¼ cup crumbled feta or queso fresco

Make the beans first. Heat the regular olive oil in a saucepan over medium heat and sauté the onion and bell pepper until the onion softens. Add the garlic and cumin and cook for another two minutes. Add the stock, orange juice, and seasoning and cook over low heat until the vegetables are tender. Add the beans, season, heat through, and add the lime juice.

Toast the bread and rub it with the garlic. Drizzle with a little of the extra virgin olive oil, then scoop out the avocado flesh and spread it coarsely on top. Season, drizzle with the rest of the extra virgin olive oil, squeeze on some lime juice, and scatter with chiles and scallions. Top with the black beans and serve with sour cream and cilantro, sprinkling with the cheese.

warm eggs, roast tomatoes & watercress cream

I LOVE THE DIFFERENT temperatures here: warm toast and eggs; tomatoes at room temperature; cold watercress cream. When pushed— and when tomatoes are good—I make this with raw tomatoes. It's really important that the egg yolks are still just a bit soft in the center and that you crush and eat the eggs while they're still warm.

SERVES 4

8 large eggs

½ cup mayonnaise

2 tablespoons sour cream or crème fraîche

1oz watercress, coarse stalks removed, finely chopped

½ teaspoon Dijon mustard

squeeze of lemon juice

4 slices of sourdough bread

unsalted butter

salt and pepper

1 quantity of Roast tomatoes (see page 54), made without harissa

Boil the eggs for seven minutes; they should still be a little soft in the center.

Meanwhile, make the watercress cream. Put the mayonnaise, cream, watercress, mustard, and lemon juice into a small food processor and whizz. Or, if you don't have a small food processor, just finely chop the watercress and mix it with the other ingredients.

Toast the bread. Drain the eggs and plunge them into cold water. As soon as they are just cool enough to handle, peel them. Butter the toast, crush the eggs onto them, season, top with the tomatoes, and spoon on some of the watercress cream. Eat immediately.

mashed eggs with anchovy, shallots & parsley

MORE SOFT, WARM EGGS. Sometimes I leave this shallot topping raw. It's sharp and strong in flavor that way, and that's what you fancy from time to time. The cooked version—as given below—is more nuanced.

SERVES 2

2 large eggs
3 tablespoons extra virgin olive oil
½ shallot, finely sliced
3 anchovies, finely chopped
½ tablespoon finely chopped flat-leaf parsley leaves
pepper
2 slices of sourdough bread
1 garlic clove

Boil the eggs for seven minutes; they should still be a little soft in the center.

Meanwhile, heat 2 tablespoons of the olive oil in a small skillet and sauté the shallot and anchovies over medium–low heat, just to take the raw edge off the shallots. The anchovies will break down a little. Add the parsley and season with pepper.

Toast the sourdough and rub each piece with the garlic. Drizzle the remaining 1 tablespoon of olive oil over both slices.

Drain the eggs and plunge them into cold water. As soon as they are just cool enough to handle, peel them. Coarsely break up each egg on a slice of sourdough—I do it directly onto the toast—then spoon the shallot and anchovy mixture over each serving.

salmon tartare
& avocado on rye

A FAVORITE SPIN on the avo-on-toast theme. If you want to be
fancy, a dollop of sour cream and a spoonful of keta (salmon roe)
look lovely and taste gorgeous, too. Since I'm a bit of a Puritan,
I only allow that on weekends.

SERVES 2

For the tartare
5½oz salmon fillet, skinned
1 small shallot, minced
1 tablespoon finely chopped dill fronds
½ tablespoon lemon juice
2 tablespoons extra virgin olive oil (fruity
    rather than grassy)
salt and pepper

For the toast
2 slices of rye bread
1 large, ripe avocado
lemon juice
avocado oil
2 crisp fresh radishes, cut into matchsticks

Cut the salmon into small ¼-inch cubes. Put these in a bowl with everything else for the
tartare. Mix and taste, seasoning well.

Toast the rye bread. Scoop out the flesh from the avocado and mash it coarsely on the toast.
Squeeze on some lemon juice, season, and drizzle with avocado oil. Spoon some tartare on
top and scatter with the radish matchsticks.

goat cheese & roast grape tartine

CHEESE ON TOAST, FRENCH STYLE. If you're roasting grapes for this, you might as well roast a larger amount. They are lovely in a salad with bitter leaves, such as radicchio, crumbled Gorgonzola cheese, and toasted walnuts.

SERVES 2

5½oz seedless black grapes
1 tablespoon olive oil
½ tablespoon balsamic vinegar
2 slices of sourdough bread
4½oz spreadable goat cheese
1½ tablespoons extra virgin olive oil
pepper
1½ tablespoons walnuts, toasted (see page 112)
a little honey (optional)
dressed salad leaves, to serve

Preheat the oven to 400°F.

Put the grapes on a baking pan and drizzle with the regular olive oil and the vinegar. Bake for 15 to 20 minutes.

Lightly toast the sourdough, but don't let it turn too golden as you are going to broil it further. Spread the goat cheese thickly on the toast, then drizzle with the extra virgin olive oil and season with pepper. Put the grapes on top and broil for two minutes, or until the cheese is golden in patches. Scatter with the walnuts and drizzle with a little honey (if using). Serve immediately with some leaves on the side.

PULSES

cumin-roast eggplants, chickpeas, walnuts & dates

THIS IS SO EASY. Stick the vegetables in the oven, make the dressing, heat the chickpeas, and voilà. It's great with couscous, but also makes a fabulous side dish for roast lamb or grilled mackerel.

SERVES 4

For the eggplant
3 eggplants, about 1lb 10oz in total
3 smallish onions
⅓ cup olive oil, divided
1 tablespoon ground cumin
2 teaspoons Aleppo pepper
salt and pepper
14oz can of chickpeas, drained and rinsed
good squeeze of lemon juice
¼oz cilantro leaves, chopped
1½ tablespoons date syrup

5 fat sticky dates, such as Medjool, pitted
  and chopped
2 tablespoons walnut pieces, toasted
  (see page 112)

For the dressing
3 tablespoons tahini
3 tablespoons extra virgin olive oil
1 fat garlic clove, crushed
¼ cup Greek yogurt
juice of ½ lemon

Preheat the oven to 375°F. Cut the eggplants horizontally into slices about ¾ inch thick, then halve the larger slices. Halve the onions and cut into crescent-shaped wedges. Put the eggplants and onions into a roasting pan, drizzle with 5 tablespoons of the regular olive oil and add the cumin, Aleppo pepper, and some seasoning. Mix it all together and roast for 45 minutes, tossing everything around every so often. The eggplants will shrink a lot. For the dressing, put everything into a blender with 3 tablespoons of water and blend. It should be the consistency of pourable thick cream. Add more water if it is too thick, then check the seasoning.

When the eggplant slices are nearly cooked, heat the remaining regular olive oil in a skillet and warm the chickpeas through. Season, add a squeeze of lemon juice, and tip into a broad, shallow bowl. Stir the cilantro into the eggplant mixture and pile on top. Drizzle with the dressing, then with the date syrup. Scatter with the dates and nuts to serve.

simple red lentil & pumpkin dal

SIMPLE TO WHIP UP ANY TIME, as long as you have some pumpkin lying around (though I've also used a mixture of carrots and parsnips when desperate and very good it was, too). Proper dals (Indian lentil stews) are finished with a "tarka"—a last-minute seasoning of fried spices and, sometimes, curry leaves—but when I'm in a hurry I forego this.

SERVES 6

3 tablespoons canola or sunflower oil, divided
1 large onion, minced
4¼ cups peeled cubed sweet pumpkin or butternut squash
1 cup chopped tomatoes
3 garlic cloves, crushed

2 teaspoons chili flakes
1¼-inch piece ginger root, peeled and grated
2 teaspoons ground cumin
½ teaspoon ground turmeric
1¼ cups red lentils
salt and pepper
3 tablespoons chopped cilantro leaves (optional)

Heat half the oil in a heavy saucepan and fry the onion until it is golden brown. Heat the rest of the oil in a skillet and sauté the pumpkin until the pieces are golden all over.

Add the tomatoes to the onion and cook for another four minutes, then add the garlic and spices and cook for two minutes, stirring a little. Add the lentils and pumpkin to the onions and pour in 4 cups of water. Season (this needs plenty of salt) and bring to a boil. Reduce the heat and cook for 20 minutes, until the lentils have collapsed and the pumpkin is tender. The mixture should be thick.

Check the seasoning. Serve scattered with cilantro, if you like. Eat with rice or flatbread and offer yogurt on the side.

breton tuna & white bean gratin

A GREAT KITCHEN-CUPBOARD RECIPE that's much more delicious than you might expect, as well as rich and satisfying. You don't need any starch on the side, just a green vegetable or salad. Ideally, you want a 7-ounce can of tuna but they can be hard to find, so a 5¾-ounce can will do.

SERVES 4

½ tablespoon olive oil

1 onion, minced

6 garlic cloves, finely sliced

2 x 14oz cans of haricot beans

salt and pepper

2 tablespoons heavy cream

2 tablespoons milk

7oz or 5¾oz can of tuna in olive oil
  (see above)

1 small dried red chile, crumbled (optional)

¼ cup grated Gruyère cheese, divided

2 tablespoons coarse white bread crumbs

1 tablespoon unsalted butter

½ tablespoon chopped parsley leaves

Preheat the oven to 350°F.

Heat the olive oil in a skillet and sauté the onion until soft but not colored (about five minutes). Add the garlic and cook for another four minutes or so. Drain one of the cans of beans and add them to the pan, then add the other with its juices (the juices are good for texture). Season really well and place over low heat so that the beans can meld with the onion.

Put the mixture into a food processor and blend to a purée. Add the cream and milk and whizz again. Tip into a bowl and add the tuna along with the oil in which it's canned, the chile, if using, and half the cheese. Stir together and taste for seasoning.

Scrape the mixture into a small gratin dish. Sprinkle with the bread crumbs and the rest of the cheese. Put little nuggets of butter all over the crumbs and bake for 20 minutes, scattering it with the parsley five minutes before the end. The gratin should be golden and bubbling; if it isn't, cook it for five minutes longer.

Serve with a green vegetable, such as broccoli.

indian sweet potatoes with chickpeas & coconut

A WONDERFUL DISH FOR A CROWD. You just need yogurt, rice, and chutney on the side. Use pumpkin instead of sweet potatoes, or replace some of the sweet potatoes with regular potatoes (round red or round white are best), if you prefer. You can get unsweetened coconut chips from health food stores (or see page 330), but omit them if you can't find them.

SERVES 8

2 tablespoons peanut oil

2 large onions, coarsely chopped

3 teaspoons ground cumin

2½ teaspoons ground coriander

1½ teaspoons ground turmeric

1 red chile, seeded and finely chopped (or leave some seeds in if you want more heat)

1-inch piece ginger root, peeled and finely grated

3 garlic cloves, crushed

bunch of cilantro, leaves and stalks separated

8 tomatoes, coarsely chopped

3 sweet potatoes, peeled and cut into chunks

salt and pepper

3 x 5¼fl oz cans of coconut cream

14oz can of chickpeas, drained and rinsed

14oz spinach, any coarse stalks removed

juice of ½ to 1 lime

handful of dried, unsweetened coconut chips (plain or toasted)

Heat the oil in a large saucepan over medium heat and add the onions. Cook for 10 minutes, stirring occasionally, until soft and golden. Stir in the dried spices and cook for two minutes, then add the chile, ginger, garlic, finely chopped cilantro stalks, and tomatoes. Cook for five minutes, stirring from time to time.

Add the sweet potatoes and 2 cups of water, season, and bring to a boil. Reduce the heat to a simmer, cover, and cook for 10 to 15 minutes. Add the coconut cream and chickpeas, then cook for 15 to 20 minutes, stirring often, until the sweet potato is cooked and the sauce thickened.

Stir in the spinach and allow it to wilt; it will only take a few minutes. Add the lime juice and taste for seasoning. Chop the cilantro leaves and scatter them on with the coconut chips.

baked merguez with beans, eggs & feta

THIS IS AN EASY MEAL—and looks great—but you need to get the sauce right, adjusting its consistency around the sausages by cooking it a little longer if you need it to be thicker, or adding more water if you want it thinner. I can't be specific because it depends on the size of pan you're using, so just adjust until you get it the way you like it. Your seasoning needs to be good, too. Be assertive.

SERVES 6 GENEROUSLY

1½ tablespoons olive oil

12 merguez, or spicy lamb, sausages

1 large onion, minced

3 garlic cloves, crushed

2 x 14oz cans of cherry tomatoes

salt and pepper

¼ tablespoon dried oregano

grated nutmeg (I use nearly ½ in this)

1 tablespoon soft light brown sugar (for the tomatoes)

extra virgin olive oil

2 x 14oz cans of white beans (haricot or cannellini), drained and rinsed

14oz can of lima beans, drained and rinsed

6 large eggs

cayenne pepper

⅓ cup crumbled feta cheese

Heat the regular olive oil in a large, broad pan (mine is cast iron, 12 inches across and 2 inches deep). Quickly brown the sausages all over on high heat to get a good color, then set aside. Add the onion and cook over medium heat until soft and pale gold, then add the garlic and cook for another minute. Pour in the canned tomatoes and season really well. Sprinkle in the oregano, nutmeg, and sugar. Bring to a boil, reduce the heat, return the sausages to the pan. Add a good slug of extra virgin olive oil (it really enriches the dish), and simmer gently for about 20 minutes.

Now add both types of beans and gently stir. Add more seasoning—beans need a lot—and perhaps a little water. You want a dish that is thick, with the beans coated in tomato sauce, but the liquid will reduce as you now should cook it for another 20 minutes, over low heat, stirring gently from time to time. If it isn't thick enough, cook for a little longer. Check the seasoning.

Break the eggs on top and allow them to cook until the whites are set (you can cover the pan to speed this up). Sprinkle a little cayenne on each egg, then scatter with feta. Serve immediately.

harissa roast carrots, white beans & dill

I LOVE TO LOOK at an ingredient in a different light. After years of regarding dill as the quintessential Scandinavian herb, it was a pleasing surprise to find it's used just as much in the Middle East, Turkey, and Greece. The fresh piney-ness is gorgeous against the oily heat of harissa.

SERVES 6

For the carrots

1lb 10oz slim carrots, with green tops

1 lemon, very finely sliced (flick the seeds out),
  plus juice of ½

2 tablespoons harissa

¼ cup olive oil

2 teaspoons cumin seeds

2 garlic cloves, crushed

2 teaspoons honey

1 cup Greek yogurt

2 tablespoons extra virgin olive oil, plus more
  to serve

¼ cup buttermilk, or whole milk

For the beans

2 tablespoons olive oil

½ onion, coarsely chopped

1 garlic clove, crushed

2 x 14oz cans of haricot or cannellini beans,
  drained and rinsed

about ¼ cup chicken or vegetable stock

salt and pepper

3 to 4 tablespoons extra virgin olive oil

good squeeze of lemon juice

½oz dill fronds, plus 1 tablespoon to serve

Preheat the oven to 400°F. Trim the carrots, leaving green tufts. If the carrots are chunky, halve lengthwise. Put into a roasting pan in a single layer (but without masses of room, or the juices burn). Add the lemon slices. Mix the harissa, regular olive oil, cumin, garlic, honey, and lemon juice and toss with the carrots. Roast for 30 to 35 minutes, turning them over once, until tender. For the beans, heat the regular olive oil in a saucepan and gently cook the onion until soft but not colored. Add the garlic, beans, stock, and seasoning. Cook over medium heat for two minutes. Stir in the extra virgin olive oil and lemon juice, then the dill. Taste for seasoning.

Mix the yogurt with the extra virgin olive oil, buttermilk or milk, and seasoning. Put the beans into a dish with the carrots and lemon slices on top. Spoon a little yogurt over (serve the rest on the side), then scatter with the 1 tablespoon of dill. Pour a little extra virgin olive oil on top to serve.

canned love

WE'RE ALL SUPPOSED TO eat fresh and seasonal these days, and cook from scratch. I'm always preaching it. But there is a shelf in my larder that I wholeheartedly love (it's my favorite shelf to organize). It is stacked with cans. And these are not standbys. Canned tomatoes are a total necessity and nobody thinks you shouldn't use them because Italians do it, too, right? But there's a very impressive supply of various canned beans and fish as well, and some of the packaging for them is so beautiful that I have to *make* myself use the contents rather than hoard them.

They're partly for emergencies because sometimes, despite my job, I forget to think about the evening meal and have to throw something together, but I like them, too. Purists may be horrified—and, weight for weight, canned beans are certainly more expensive than dried—but I use them an awful lot. No cans of cannellini beans? It's a crisis. No canned anchovies? How could I let that happen? Canned beans aren't always a good alternative to the dried variety, though. Dishes such as cassoulet—where the beans become deliciously imbued with fat, herbs, and stock as they cook for hours—are better made with dried beans. Nevertheless, I don't often have time for that kind of cooking.

Creamy canned flageolets with garlic, cream, and parsley are amazing alongside lamb chops: they're not Michelin star but they're satisfying, the kind of thing a chic-but-harassed French woman would make. Mashed canned chickpeas, the beans crushed with sautéed onions, loads of garlic, cumin, lemon juice, and a good dollop of harissa, is fantastic with purple sprouting broccoli (and I can't tell the difference between home-cooked and good canned chickpeas anyway).

A can of anchovies, chopped and gently heated in a pan with garlic, a chile, and olive oil until they melt, then finished with parsley: that can go on my pasta any day, or my fish, or even lamb chops for that matter. Even Greek baked beans—a dish that is usually made really slowly—can be perfectly delicious when made with canned beans. You just need to take care not to cook the canned beans so much that they fall apart. Treat them gently.

Opening a can and quickly throwing a dish together gives me a real buzz. I'm getting a bit of help, but I still have the fun part to do: the seasoning, the tasting. It's the kind of cooking most of us do when we start out. I didn't learn about cooking by making lobster à l'américaine; I started by using sautéed onions, bell peppers, and a can of haricots to make spicy beans.

Okay, I'm not suggesting you use canned potatoes (not even those from France), but you should feel proud of the get-it-on-the-table-quickly cooking that other cans make possible. It's about turning the ordinary into something special. So stock up with pride.

El Velero
CONSERVAS
ORTIZ
ANCHOAS en aceite de oliva
ABRE FÁCIL

FILETS DE SARDINES
SANS PEAU
les enfandines
A LA
TOMATE
Connétable
DEPUIS 1853

VINTAGE 2002
CHOICEST FISH
IN PUREST OLIVE OIL
By Special Royal Permission
KING OSCAR BRAND
BRISLING
IN PUREST OLIVE OIL

DESDE 1891
CONSERVAS
ORTIZ
El Velero
BONITO DEL NORTE
EN ACEITE DE
OLIVA

thyme-baked mushrooms & cranberry beans with roast garlic crème fraîche

ROASTED MUSHROOMS offer a big dose of umami—they're deeply meaty and savory—and you don't have to do much with them. Season, drizzle with olive oil and a little vinegar, and throw them in the oven. The beans here mute their meatiness slightly, and add an earthy sweetness. If you don't want to go to the bother of roasting the garlic, just crush a small raw garlic clove and stir it into the crème fraîche instead.

SERVES 4 as a side dish

1lb 2oz portabellini or portobello
 mushrooms, carefully wiped clean
1 large onion, cut into wedges about
 ¾ inch thick
⅓ cup olive oil, divided
2 tablespoons balsamic vinegar
8 sprigs of thyme

salt and pepper
1 small garlic bulb
1 tablespoon extra virgin olive oil, plus more to serve
14oz can of cranberry beans, drained and rinsed
juice of ½ lemon
⅔ cup crème fraîche

Preheat the oven to 400°F. If you have larger portobello mushrooms, slice thickly. Arrange the mushrooms and onion in a roasting pan in single layer. It looks a lot, but they shrink. Toss with 5 tablespoons of the regular olive oil, the vinegar, thyme, and seasoning. Cut the top off the garlic and seal the bulb into a foil parcel with a splash of water and the 1 tablespoon of extra virgin olive oil. Set on a cookie sheet. Roast the garlic and mushrooms for 45 minutes. Mushrooms throw out a lot of water, but it should evaporate; they should also be dark. When there are 10 minutes to go, heat the remaining 1 tablespoon of regular olive oil in a skillet and quickly sauté the beans. Season well. Add to the mushrooms while they finish cooking.

Toss the contents of the roasting pan. If they seem wet, set on medium–high heat and boil most of the moisture off. Tip into a warm bowl. Add the lemon and drizzle with extra virgin olive oil. Squeeze the garlic out of its skins, mash, then stir into the crème fraîche. Serve alongside.

greek baked beans with dill, preserved lemon & feta

MUCH MORE THAN the sum of its parts. It's rich, but made from humble ingredients—olive oil and slow cooking does this—and the herbs, cheese, and lemon make it special, even if preserved lemons are Moroccan, rather than Greek. Jars of cooked beans are much more expensive than canned, but they are luscious. If you want a cheaper option, use three 14-ounce cans of cannellini or lima beans (or a mixture) instead of beans from a jar.

SERVES 6 as a main course

2 tablespoons extra virgin olive oil, plus more
   to serve
1 large onion, coarsely chopped
2 medium carrots, peeled and finely chopped
2 celery stalks, finely chopped
3 garlic cloves, crushed
2 x 14oz cans of cherry tomatoes in thick juice
salt and pepper

1 to 2 teaspoons soft light brown sugar
2 teaspoons dried oregano
1 bay leaf
2 x 1lb 6oz jars of large cooked white beans
¼oz dill fronds, chopped
2/3 cup crumbled feta cheese
1 preserved lemon (½ if home-made; 1 if bought),
   fleshy parts removed, rind cut into shreds

Preheat the oven to 350°F. Heat the olive oil in a cast-iron casserole with a lid and sauté the onion, carrots, and celery until soft, but not colored. Add the garlic and cook for another few minutes. Add the tomatoes and bring to a boil, pressing the tomatoes to crush them. Simmer for about 10 minutes. Season well and stir in the sugar, oregano, bay leaf, and beans.

Cover and bake for 30 minutes, then stir and return to the oven without the lid. Bake for another 30 minutes, checking once or twice, until the liquid has reduced and the mixture is thick. Stir in a glug of oil and the dill and check the seasoning. Serve scattered with the feta cheese and preserved lemon. A bowl of yogurt is lovely on the side.

roast cauliflower with pomegranates, green olives & chickpea purée

A SALAD OF POMEGRANATES, green olives, and walnuts is common in Turkey and that's how this dish started off. If you don't want to make the chickpea purée then just toss drained chickpeas into the dish, or add cooked farro, spelt, or wheat berries to make it into a big salad (you'll need more lemon, extra virgin olive oil, and seasoning).

SERVES 4 as a main course, 6 as a side dish or mezze

For the cauliflower
florets from 1 large cauliflower
1 teaspoon cayenne pepper
1½ teaspoons cumin seeds
¼ cup olive oil
salt and pepper
⅓ cup walnuts, toasted (see page 112)
½ cup chopped green olives
leaves from a bunch of cilantro, chopped
juice of ½ to 1 lemon, to taste

about 1 tablespoon extra virgin olive oil
seeds from ½ pomegranate

For the chickpea purée
14oz can of chickpeas, drained and rinsed
1 garlic clove, crushed
1½ tablespoons tahini
1 teaspoon ground cumin
1 heaped teaspoon cayenne pepper
⅔ cup extra virgin olive oil
juice of 1 lemon, or to taste

Preheat the oven to 400°F. Put the cauliflower into a roasting pan in which it can lie in a single layer. Add the cayenne and cumin, the regular olive oil, and seasoning. Toss with your hands and then roast for 30 to 35 minutes. Toss occasionally so the cauliflower turns golden all over. Meanwhile, make the purée. Purée the chickpeas in a food processor with the garlic, tahini, cumin, and cayenne, then add the extra virgin olive oil in a steady stream. Add the lemon juice to taste. Season and add enough water to get the texture you want. Check the seasoning.

When the cauliflower is cooked, toss in the walnuts, olives, cilantro, and lemon juice. Drizzle with the extra virgin olive oil and scatter with pomegranate seeds. Serve with the purée. If this is to be a main course, couscous or bulgur wheat with chopped preserved lemons stirred into it makes a very good side dish.

lamb & bulgur pilaf with figs & preserved lemons

BULGUR PILAFS only take 20 minutes to cook. This recipe is good for using up leftover roast lamb. To avoid the expense of fresh figs (though they look and taste gorgeous), you can use 1¾oz of moist dried figs, chopped, soaked in just-boiled water for 30 minutes, then drained.

SERVES 4

3 tablespoons olive oil

8 fresh figs, stalks snipped off, halved

1lb 2oz boneless lamb (from the sirloin end), cut into chunks (or see recipe introduction)

1 large onion, coarsely chopped

¼ teaspoon chili flakes

½ teaspoon ground allspice

3 teaspoons ground cumin

1 garlic clove, crushed

1¼ cups bulgur wheat

1½ cups lamb stock

salt and pepper

3 tablespoons raisins

½ x 14oz can of chickpeas, drained and rinsed

¼ cup walnut pieces, toasted (see page 112)

2 tablespoons chopped flat-leaf parsley and cilantro leaves

2 preserved lemons (1 if home-made; 2 if bought), fleshy parts removed, rind cut into shreds

Heat 1½ tablespoons of the olive oil in a sauté pan and, when it's really hot, quickly cook the figs, cut-side down first, until they are tender and golden on the cut side. Remove and set aside.

Add the rest of the oil and brown the lamb in two batches over high heat until it has a good color all over, taking each batch out as it is browned. Add the onion and cook for about eight minutes, first on high heat to get a decent color, then on low heat to help it soften. Stir in the chili flakes, allspice, cumin, and garlic and sauté for another two minutes. Add the bulgur wheat and stir to coat in the oily juices. Pour in the stock and add seasoning, tip in the raisins, and return the lamb. Bring to a boil, then immediately reduce the heat to low. Cover the pan and cook for 15 minutes, until the liquid has been absorbed and the bulgur is tender. Season.

Gently fork in the chickpeas. Cover again and let stand for another 10 minutes off the heat to allow the bulgur to fluff up. Gently fork through the nuts, herbs, and preserved lemons, then transfer to a heated bowl and put the figs on top. Serve with Greek yogurt on the side.

PASTA
& GRAINS

pappardelle with cavolo nero, chiles & hazelnuts

ONE OF MY FAVORITE DISHES is pasta tossed with garlic, chile, parsley, olive oil, and orange zest. I've simply added cabbage and nuts here to make it a bit healthier (and quite a lot more delicious).

SERVES 4

14oz pappardelle

salt and pepper

1lb 9oz cavolo nero

⅓ cup extra virgin olive oil, plus more to serve

3 garlic cloves, finely sliced

2 red chiles, seeded and chopped, or about ½ teaspoon chili flakes

finely grated zest of ½ large orange

⅓ cup hazelnuts, halved and toasted (see page 281)

scant 1oz flat-leaf parsley leaves, coarsely chopped

finely grated Parmesan cheese, to serve

Put the pasta in a large pan of boiling salted water and cook until al dente, about 15 minutes, or a minute or so less than suggested on the package directions. Meanwhile, remove the tough ribs from the cavolo nero (discard them) and wash the leaves. Plunge into boiling water and cook for seven minutes. Drain well. Squeeze the excess water from the cabbage with your hands and chop it coarsely.

When the pasta has about four minutes left to cook, heat the oil and gently sauté the garlic and chile until the garlic is pale gold. Add the zest and cabbage, season well, and heat through.

Drain the pasta, return it to its pan, and add the hazelnuts and the contents of the cabbage pan. Season and add the parsley. Drizzle with more olive oil. Serve with grated Parmesan cheese.

new york takeout noodles with cucumber

SOMETHING TO TURN TO when you're tired and the cupboard is pretty
bare. You can eat it with hot spiced meat—grilled chicken or pork—or just
chow down with the noodles in front of the television. The recipe is from *The
New York Times* and is based on a dish made by Shorty Tang at the Hwa Yuan
restaurant on East Broadway. As with many Asian dishes, the art is in balance.
The sesame sauce needs to be hot, sweet, salty, and a tiny bit sour. Sometimes I
add sliced radishes to the cucumber, soaking the radishes in iced water to give
a really good crunch; it's a great contrast to the soft noodles. There are lots of
chile-garlic pastes on the market and they vary a lot in heat, so add it to taste.
I prefer to use a Chinese variety for this, such as Sichuan chile bean paste, but
you could also use sriracha (see page 330 for suppliers).

SERVES 6

1lb 9oz medium egg noodles

2 tablespoons toasted sesame oil, plus extra

2 tablespoons Chinese sesame paste
  (see page 330)

1½ tablespoons smooth peanut butter

3½ tablespoons dark soy sauce

2 tablespoons rice vinegar

1 tablespoon soft light brown sugar

½-inch piece ginger root, peeled and finely grated

1 fat garlic clove, finely grated

chile-garlic paste, to taste (it should be hot)

1 cucumber, peeled and very finely sliced

handful of roasted salted peanuts, chopped

handful of chopped herb leaves, such as mint
  and cilantro

Cook the noodles following the package directions, then drain and rinse in cold water. Shake
off the excess water in a colander. Put the noodles into a bowl and drizzle with a little toasted
sesame oil to stop them from sticking together.

Whisk the sesame paste and peanut butter in a bowl (just use a fork), then whisk in the soy
sauce, rice vinegar, the 2 tablespoons of sesame oil, sugar, ginger, garlic, and chile-garlic paste.
Taste and adjust if you need to. It might seem strong, but it's going onto bland noodles. Toss
the sauce with the noodles and top with the cucumber, then add the peanuts and herbs.

crab & peas
with casarecce

FOR A RICHER DISH, add 3 tablespoons of cream to the crab before
you toss it with the pasta. The brown crab meat here intensifies the
flavor, even if it does make it look "muddy," but it's optional. I like
the shape of casarecce, but you can use other pasta instead.

SERVES 4

5½oz casarecce, or other pasta shapes

salt and pepper

3½oz sugar snap peas

1 cup fresh or frozen peas

2 tablespoons unsalted butter

1 tablespoon olive oil

2 garlic cloves, finely sliced

9¾oz white crab meat, picked over

1¾oz brown crab meat (optional)

a couple of generous squeezes of lemon juice

¾oz pea shoots, coarse stalks removed

Cook the pasta in plenty of boiling lightly salted water until tender but still al dente (this is
usually a couple of minutes less than suggested on the package).

Halve the sugar snap peas lengthwise so you can see the peas peeking out. Put these and the
regular peas into a saucepan of boiling water and cook for about two minutes. Meanwhile,
heat the butter and oil in a small skillet and cook the garlic until it's soft. Toss in the crab
meat, including the brown meat, if using, and briskly heat. Add salt, pepper, and a good
squeeze of lemon juice.

Drain the pasta and put it into a warm serving bowl with the drained peas, the crab, and
all the juices from its pan and the pea shoots. Toss together gently—don't crush the pea
shoots—season again, add another good squeeze of lemon juice, and serve.

orzo with lemon & parsley

I CAN'T TELL YOU HOW USEFUL this is. When I feel lazy, I make it instead of risotto. It takes—literally—12 minutes from beginning to end. The result is a creamy dish that is very soothing on its own, or lovely with roast or grilled chicken. Orzo is a pasta that looks like grains of rice. If you're a Parmesan cheese lover you'll adore it, as orzo is pretty much a vehicle for the stuff. Orzo is also great to feed to hungry children because it cooks so quickly and, when you're ill, it's like Italian penicillin in a bowl. It's also the most terrific television food; snuggle into your sofa with a bowl and eat with a spoon. You can add chopped spinach to this as well. It will just wilt in the heat of the pasta.

SERVES 4 as a side dish, 2 as a main course
½ tablespoon olive oil
4 shallots or ½ small onion, minced
1 garlic clove, minced
1¾ cups light chicken stock
8oz orzo
finely grated zest of ½ unwaxed lemon
3 tablespoons finely chopped parsley leaves
¾ to 1 cup finely grated Parmesan cheese, to taste
salt and pepper

Heat the olive oil and gently sauté the shallots until soft and pale gold. Add the garlic and cook for a further couple of minutes. Add the stock and bring to a boil, then add the orzo.

Increase the heat to medium and cook, uncovered, for eight minutes. You can stir it a couple of times to stop the pasta from sticking, but try not to do so too much. By the end the stock should have been absorbed and the pasta become soft, but still with a little firmness.

Stir in the lemon zest, parsley, and Parmesan cheese. Taste and season; you won't need much salt, if any, because of the reduced stock and the cheese. Eat promptly; it gets sticky if it's kept waiting, although it does—amazingly—reheat well if you do it gently with a little more stock.

fettuccine with asparagus, peas & saffron

RATHER CHIC, and something of a treat if there are just two of you. Shreds of Parma ham, flaked cooked salmon, or—if you're pushing the boat out—seared scallops are all lovely additions. Just toss them with the cream and the vegetables.

SERVES 2

generous pinch of saffron stamens

1 tablespoon unsalted butter

2 shallots, minced

3½fl oz vermouth

1 cup chicken or vegetable stock

½ cup heavy cream

salt and pepper

lemon juice

6oz fresh fettuccine

7oz asparagus tips

1¼ cups peas

finely grated Parmesan or pecorino cheese, to serve

Put the saffron in a cup and stir in 3 tablespoons of boiling water. Set aside for 30 minutes.

For the sauce, melt the butter in a saucepan and cook the shallots until soft but not colored. Add the vermouth and boil until it has reduced to about 3 tablespoons. Add the saffron water and stock and boil until reduced by two-thirds. Add the cream and bring to a boil. Season and boil until the sauce can coat the back of a spoon. Add a little lemon juice and check the seasoning.

Cook the pasta in boiling lightly salted water until al dente, about a minute or so less than suggested on the package directions. When it is nearly ready, steam the asparagus tips until just tender (test with the tip of a knife), boil the peas for three minutes, and drain. Drain the pasta and toss quickly with the vegetables and sauce. Serve with grated Parmesan or pecorino cheese.

turkish pasta with feta, yogurt & dill

TURKISH MANTI—lamb-filled pasta shapes—are served with yogurt sauce. They're laborious to make, but I love the basic idea of pasta with yogurt and feta and so I came up with this instead. It takes a while for the onions to caramelize but you can pretty much leave them to cook.

SERVES 2

4 medium onions (about 1lb), very finely sliced

2 tablespoons olive oil

1 bay leaf

2-inch piece of cinnamon stick

1 garlic clove, crushed

salt and pepper

1 teaspoon superfine sugar (optional)

squeeze of lemon juice (optional)

5¼oz tagliatelle

3 tablespoons Greek yogurt

1½ tablespoons milk or buttermilk

2 tablespoons chopped dill fronds

1 tablespoon unsalted butter

¼ teaspoon cayenne pepper

finely crumbled feta cheese, to serve

Put the onions in a heavy pan with the olive oil, bay, and cinnamon. Cook over medium heat, stirring, until the onions are starting to turn golden, then add the garlic and cook for a further two minutes. Add a splash of water, cover the pan, reduce the heat right down, and let cook until the onions are almost caramelized, about 35 minutes. Check on them every so often to give them a stir and ensure they're not getting too dry.

When the onions are totally soft, remove the lid, season, and boil until any excess liquid has evaporated. (If they haven't caramelized very well you could add the 1 teaspoon of sugar, but balance it by adding a good squeeze of lemon juice, too.)

Cook the tagliatelle until al dente in boiling salted water, usually a couple of minutes less than suggested on the package. When it is almost ready, add the yogurt and milk or buttermilk to the onions and heat, but don't boil. Drain the pasta and toss it into the onion pan with the dill.

Quickly melt the butter in a small saucepan and add the cayenne. Cook for about 20 seconds. Serve the pasta with the spiced butter drizzled on top and offer the feta cheese on the side.

black linguine with squid & spicy sausage

BLACK PASTA is easier to find than it was. Its main advantage is that it looks so dramatic, especially if you serve something white—squid, shrimp, or scallops—with it (all are good here), but you can of course use regular pasta. Don't add too much parsley, as it can dominate. Look for spicy Italian sausages in a good deli, though supermarkets sell spicy sausages, usually smoky Spanish-flavored varieties, which work, too.

SERVES 2

5½oz black linguine or spaghetti
salt and pepper
10½oz squid, cleaned
5½oz spicy sausage
3 tablespoons olive oil, divided
2 garlic cloves, finely sliced

1 red chile, seeded and finely chopped
1 tablespoon finely chopped flat-leaf parsley leaves
juice of ½ lemon
extra virgin olive oil, to serve

Cook the pasta in plenty of boiling lightly salted water following the package directions. Meanwhile, get on with the squid and sausage.

Cut the wings off the squid. If they are large, cut them into three or four strips, but it's usually fine just to halve them. Slice the bodies down one side, then cut into ½-inch strips. Separate the tentacles, halving if they're big. Blot the squid with paper towels: if it's wet it won't fry well.

Remove the casing from the sausage and break the meat into little nuggets a bit bigger than a pea. Heat 1 tablespoon of the regular olive oil in a large skillet or a wok and cook the sausagemeat over fairly high heat until browned all over. Lift out with a slotted spoon and set aside. Add the rest of the regular olive oil and increase the heat to high. When it is very hot, throw in the squid and cook for about a minute, then add the garlic, chile, seasoning, and the sausage. Toss it around for another 30 to 40 seconds (you want the garlic to be pale gold, but not to burn).

Throw in the parsley and squeeze on the lemon juice. Quickly drain the pasta and add it to the pan. Toss everything around, add a good slug of extra virgin olive oil, and serve immediately.

linguine all'amalfitana

I'M ALWAYS LOOKING for new simple pasta dishes and southern Italy is a great hunting ground. Anchovies and walnuts seems like an odd pairing, but it works well.

SERVES 2

5¾oz linguine

salt and pepper

3 tablespoons extra virgin olive oil, plus more to serve (optional)

2 garlic cloves, crushed

½ teaspoon chili flakes

⅓ cup walnuts, coarsely chopped

8 really good-quality cured anchovies, coarsely chopped

finely grated pecorino cheese, to serve (optional)

Cook the linguine in boiling salted water until al dente, usually a couple of minutes less than it says on the package directions.

Meanwhile, heat the olive oil in a sauté pan or a shallow cast-iron casserole and gently fry the garlic, chili flakes, and nuts for a few minutes. Don't let the garlic brown. Add the anchovies and press them down in the pan with the back of a wooden spoon; they'll melt in the heat.

Add ¾ cup of the pasta cooking water to the anchovy pan, then drain the pasta and add that to the pan, too. Cook the pasta in the sauté pan for a couple of minutes. The cooking water will reduce to form a sauce with the other ingredients and the pasta will become glossy. Season.

You can add another slug of extra virgin olive oil, if you want. Serve with grated pecorino cheese, or without any cheese at all.

pasta all'ortolana

VERY CLEVER THIS: basically a carbonara made with zucchini. I use a fairly high proportion of vegetables to pasta because I like it that way, but increase the quantity of spaghetti if you want.

SERVES 4

10½oz spaghetti

salt and pepper

14oz zucchini

¼ cup extra virgin olive oil

1 small onion, very finely sliced

1 garlic clove, very finely sliced

2 eggs, plus 4 egg yolks

1 cup finely grated Parmesan cheese

½ cup finely grated pecorino cheese

leaves from a small bunch of basil, torn

Cook the spaghetti in a large pan of boiling lightly salted water until it is al dente (usually a couple of minutes less than it says on the package).

Meanwhile, trim off the tops and bases of the zucchini and cut the flesh into strips (somewhere between matchsticks and batons). Heat the olive oil in a large skillet and sauté the zucchini and onion over medium–high heat (you'll need to reduce it after a while), until golden all over and cooked through. Add the garlic and cook for another minute.

In a bowl, beat the eggs, yolks, and both cheeses well, seasoning with lots of pepper.

When the pasta is al dente, drain, reserving ½ cup of the cooking water. Pour the reserved pasta water into the zucchini. Now add the spaghetti to the pan and stir it with the vegetables, leaving it on the heat for a few moments to allow some of the water to evaporate and the pasta to absorb the flavors.

Working quickly, take the pan off the heat and stir in the egg and cheese mixture, moving everything around until every strand of pasta is coated and the sauce has thickened. The eggs shouldn't scramble, but the sauce should just thicken instead. Taste. Add more salt if it needs it, throw on the basil, and serve immediately.

pâtes à la cévenole

THIS RECIPE IS FROM SOUTHERN FRANCE and, if you like comforting bowls of pasta, it's a stunner. Don't be put off by the chestnuts; they really make the dish. You can buy them frozen or vacuum-packed.

SERVES 6

7oz small macaroni

salt and pepper

14oz cremino mushrooms, or other mushrooms if you can't find those

1 tablespoon olive oil

1 tablespoon unsalted butter

½ garlic clove, minced

4½oz cooked chestnuts, very coarsely chopped

2 cups heavy cream

freshly grated nutmeg

¾ cup Gruyère cheese, grated

Put the macaroni into a large pot of boiling lightly salted water and cook until al dente (usually a couple of minutes less than it says on the package). Preheat the oven to 375°F.

Get on with the rest of the dish while the pasta is cooking. Slice the mushrooms quite thickly and sauté them in the olive oil over fairly high heat until golden brown. You want a good color here. (You may have to do it in batches as there are a lot of mushrooms.) They throw out a lot of water and you have to drive this off, or you'll end up with gray liquid when the dish is baked.

Add the butter to the mushrooms—it's great for flavor—plus the garlic, chestnuts, and seasoning. Drain the pasta and add it, too. Pour in the cream, grate in the nutmeg (be generous), and bring to a boil. Check the seasoning again.

Transfer immediately to a gratin dish and scatter the cheese on top. Cook in the oven for 45 minutes. It should be golden and bubbling and the cream should have reduced. Serve with a baby spinach or watercress salad.

pasta master

AUGUST IN ROME. I'm sitting in a quiet trattoria in the suburbs. It has taken an hour to get here in the sweltering heat but it's worth it. This place is famous for its fritti—arancini, zucchini flowers stuffed with cheese and anchovies—and its pasta.

As soon as the carbonara, a dish in which eggs are cooked just enough by strands of hot spaghetti to form a "sauce" (but not so much that they scramble) arrives, I am completely content. I'm also reminded how good something this ordinary and inexpensive—only the nuggets of salty guanciale with which the dish is studded cost much—can be. It isn't just the flavor, it's the fact that it's soft, that there is a ritual to eating it—twirling it around your fork—that it can be made quickly, and with a little style.

I watch the Italians around me eating small platefuls of pasta as a precursor to their *pollo alla diavola* or veal chop and think of my favorite pasta photographs, of Maria Callas and a group of her girlfriends eating pasta on a train in 1955 on the way to La Scala, of Sophia Loren looking for all the world as if pasta had created every wonderful curve on her body. They are all eating with such joy, heads held back, and mouths wide open, as though a love of pasta exhibits a love of life itself.

Most of us, in contrast, have come to regard pasta not as a joy, but as a filler. It's the convenience food par excellence; it's easy and nearly every child will eat it. God knows what we did before supermarkets were full of packages of tubes, strands, shells, corkscrews, and butterflies. Familiarity has, to a certain extent, bred contempt.

For a start, we don't prepare it well. Pasta has to be cooked in plenty of boiling salted water (4 cups for every 3½ ounces of pasta). Dress it with melted butter or olive oil if your sauce isn't ready and, when saucing, don't overdo it because the pasta, with its own flavor and texture, is just as important as the sauce. Remember that the sauce should just coat the pasta, not drown it. Adding a little of the cooking water from the pasta to the sauce loosens it, and helps both pasta and sauce to combine well.

Tossed with cream, lemon zest, and shreds of Parma ham, or with wild mushrooms and truffles, pasta can be luxurious, but more often it allows you to revel in the frugal and also to cook spontaneously. I feel a little rise of pleasure as I spot a bunch of parsley that can be tossed with spaghetti, extra virgin olive oil, and dried chiles. Carrying a big bowl of this to the table makes me happy: I've taken ordinary ingredients and turned them into something good.

Frugal, simple, generous, these are some of the best attributes a dish can have (in my book, anyway). Pasta, if cooked with care and approached with verve, can be all these things, something that Maria Callas and Sophia Loren knew well.

smoky couscous

You can extend this: add cooked chickpeas or black beans, sautéing them in a little olive oil if you want to serve the dish hot; or baby spinach. It's great with pork (try it with Spanish spiced pork with sherried onions, see page 170), lamb, or "meaty" fish such as monkfish. I also like it with fried tomatoes and chopped chiles tossed in, topped with a fried egg. Couscous is not a grain—it's made from little pellets of rolled semolina—but is treated as one, which is why it is in this chapter. It's a boon, as it's so quick to prepare. And the riffs on it (it goes as well with cool dill as with hot chiles and smoky paprika) are endless.

Serves 6 to 8 as a side dish

1¼ cups couscous

1¼ cups boiling chicken or vegetable stock, or just boiling water

¼ cup olive oil, divided

1 large onion, very finely sliced

2 garlic cloves, minced

1½ teaspoons smoked paprika

juice of ½ lemon

2 tablespoons extra virgin olive oil

⅓ cup pitted green olives, coarsely chopped

2½ tablespoons smoked almonds, coarsely chopped

a few roasted red bell peppers from a jar, torn or chopped (optional)

leaves from a small bunch of cilantro, chopped

salt and pepper

Sprinkle the couscous into a bowl, pour the hot stock or water over it, and add half the regular olive oil. Cover with plastic wrap and let stand for 15 minutes.

Heat the remaining regular olive oil in a skillet and sauté the onion over medium heat until soft and golden. Add the garlic and smoked paprika and cook for a further minute.

Fork the couscous through. It should be fluffy, and not wet (if it is dry, add no more than 3 tablespoons extra stock or water and let it stand for a little longer). Fork the onion mixture into the couscous. Add the lemon juice, extra virgin olive oil, olives, almonds, bell peppers (if using), and cilantro. Season.

Gently toss together and serve warm or at room temperature.

spelt with blackberries, beets, walnuts & buttermilk

I STARTED OUT MAKING a Scandinavian-influenced dish here—spelt, berries, and buttermilk are such northern ingredients—but I went off on another tack, adding spices and heat. You can leave the spices out—or use more Scandi flavors, caraway for example—depending on what you want to serve it with. It's surprisingly good with salmon and mackerel.

SERVES 6 TO 8 as a side dish

1 cup pearled spelt
2½ tablespoons olive oil, divided
juice of ½ lemon
1 teaspoon white balsamic vinegar
salt and pepper
½ red onion, very finely sliced
1 teaspoon ground coriander
1 teaspoon cayenne pepper
¼ cup walnut pieces
2 cooked beets, cut into matchsticks

1 cup blackberries
1 tablespoon chopped dill fronds
1 tablespoon chopped cilantro leaves

For the dressing
1 cup buttermilk
smidgen of Dijon mustard
pinch of superfine sugar
1 garlic clove, crushed
2 tablespoons extra virgin olive oil

Cook the spelt in boiling water until tender (20 to 25 minutes, but check the package directions). Drain and run cold water through it. Shake off the excess water and add to a serving bowl with 2 tablespoons of the regular olive oil, the lemon juice, vinegar and seasoning.

Make the buttermilk dressing by mixing everything together. Taste for seasoning.

Heat the rest of the regular olive oil and cook the onion until it has just lost its rawness, then add the spices and cook for another two minutes. Add this to the spelt, then toast the walnut pieces in the same pan for a minute or so, until they smell aromatic. Tip them into the bowl along with all the other ingredients and gently toss together.

Drizzle with some of the buttermilk dressing (offer the rest in a small pitcher) and serve.

eastern black rice, mango & tomatoes with coconut

BLACK "VENUS" RICE—I apologize for the high-falutin' name—is a new discovery for me. It's not like sticky Asian black rice, as the grains stay separate and nutty. I adore it. It looks spectacular with bright colors. You can get the coconut flesh for this in little cartons now, so you don't have to buy a whole coconut.

SERVES 6 TO 8 as a side dish

For the salad
1½ cups black "venus" rice
1 mango, just ripe or slightly under-ripe
3½oz sugar snap peas
½oz basil leaves
leaves from 10 sprigs of mint
½lb well flavored tomatoes, chopped
2 red and 1 green chile, seeded and shredded
2 scallions, trimmed and finely chopped
3½ tablespoons chopped roasted salted peanuts
1½oz fresh coconut flesh, shaved

For the dressing
finely grated zest and juice of 2 limes
1 garlic clove, finely grated
¾-inch piece ginger root, peeled
    and finely grated
2 tablespoons peanut oil
1½ tablespoons fish sauce
2½ tablespoons superfine sugar

Put the rice into a saucepan of boiling water, then reduce the heat to a good, vigorous simmer. Cook until tender, though it retains a "bite." It takes about 45 minutes. Drain and rinse under cold water until the water runs clear. This rice stains, so you need to get the excess color out.

Peel the mango and cut the "cheeks" off each side (the parts lying right next to the seed). Cut really close to the seed so that you remove the plumpest bit of the mango you can. Carefully remove the other bits of flesh; you can't use any here that is soft or bruised, so reserve that for a smoothie. Cut into chunks about ½-inch square.

Shred the sugar snaps lengthwise. To make the dressing, just mix everything together; it will taste quite tart. Tear the larger basil and mint leaves, leaving the small leaves intact.

Gently mix the dressing with all the ingredients, except the peanuts and coconut, in a broad shallow bowl where you can see all the colors. Scatter with the peanuts and coconut and serve.

smoked haddock, barley & spinach salad

IF YOU WANT to make this more substantial, a poached egg is lovely on top. Spelt or farro can be used instead of barley; just cook them in the same way.

SERVES 6

For the dressing
1 tablespoon Dijon mustard
¼ cup white wine vinegar
salt and pepper
1 teaspoon superfine sugar
¾ cup light and fruity
    extra virgin olive oil
⅓ cup light cream

For the salad
1 cup pearl barley
2 tablespoons olive oil
good squeeze of lemon juice
1 tablespoon chopped parsley leaves
2¼lb undyed smoked haddock fillet,
    cut into 6 portions
2 tablespoons unsalted butter
1 tablespoon sunflower oil
¾lb baby spinach

To make the dressing, put the mustard, vinegar, seasoning, and sugar into a small pitcher and gradually add the extra virgin olive oil, whisking with a fork as you do so. Whisk in the cream and taste for seasoning. Set aside.

Cook the barley in boiling lightly salted water until tender, about 30 minutes. Drain, rinse in warm water, and drain again, shaking out any excess liquid. Transfer to a warm bowl and stir in the regular olive oil, lemon juice, parsley, and seasoning. Cover and keep warm.

Make sure there are no little bones in the fish by rubbing your hands over the surface. Divide the butter and sunflower oil between two skillets and cook three pieces of fish in each, flesh-side down first, over medium heat until pale gold underneath (about two minutes). Carefully turn the fish over, reduce the heat a little, and cover both pans. Cook for about five minutes, or until the flesh is opaque. Remove the pans from the heat.

Divide the spinach among six plates with the barley. Lift the fish from its skin—I use a knife and fork—trying to keep it in fairly big chunks. Put it on the salad and spoon over the dressing.

spelt with carrots & kale

SIDE DISHES get a rather bad deal in cookbooks, though an array of good sides are a real boon. Use cavolo nero if you prefer it to kale.

SERVES 6 as a side dish

2 tablespoons unsalted butter, divided

1 small onion, minced

3 carrots, peeled and finely chopped

1¾ cups pearled spelt

2½ cups light chicken stock

10½oz kale, coarse ribs discarded, leaves coarsely chopped

salt and pepper

Melt 1 tablespoon of the butter in a saucepan and add the onion and carrots. Sauté over medium heat until soft but not colored. Add the spelt and stir around in the fat. Pour in the stock, bring to a boil, then reduce the heat to a simmer. Gently simmer for about 30 minutes. It will become tender—though it will retain a little "bite" in the middle of each grain—and should have absorbed all the stock. Take off the heat and cover to keep warm.

Put the kale in a saucepan and add enough boiling water to cover. Cook for five minutes over medium heat, then drain and squeeze out any excess water with your hands. Put it into a small pan with the rest of the butter, season, and sauté for a few minutes until some of the moisture has evaporated. Stir into the warm spelt. Serve immediately.

bacon & egg risotto

RATHER ANNOYINGLY I'm asking for 3 cups of stock here, when
supermarkets sell 2-cup containers. If you aren't using home-made
stock you can actually use a 2-cup container here and top off the
remaining quantity with water. You're reducing the stock as it cooks
in the risotto, so you'll still end up with a good flavor. If you like
the comfort of poached eggs (and who doesn't?) you will love this.
Poached eggs + risotto = bliss.

SERVES 2
3 cups chicken stock
1 tablespoon unsalted butter
5½oz bacon lardons
1 small onion, minced
¾ cup risotto rice
pepper
2 tablespoons finely chopped parsley leaves
¼ cup finely grated Parmesan cheese, divided
2 eggs

Heat the stock and keep it simmering while you cook the risotto.

Melt the butter in a heavy saucepan and sauté the bacon until golden all over, then stir in the
onion. Cook over medium heat until the onion is soft and pale gold. Add the rice, turning it
over in the fat and juices, and cook for a couple of minutes until it is translucent.

Add the stock a ladle at a time, stirring continuously. Don't add any new stock until the last lot
has been absorbed. The rice will soften and become creamy with just a little bite in the center of
each grain. It takes 20 to 25 minutes. Season with pepper (you shouldn't need salt because of the
bacon and stock). Stir in the parsley and half the Parmesan cheese and check the seasoning.

Cover and let rest while you quickly poach the eggs (see page 19, or poach them according
to your favorite method). Serve an egg on top of each serving of risotto with the remaining
Parmesan cheese on the side.

couscous with flowers

DISHES LIKE THIS ARE MAGICAL because you've made some effort
with your shopping, not with your cooking. Farmer's markets often have
stands selling edible flowers and petals, so see what you can find. Other
edible flowers, such as geraniums, nasturtiums, and roses can be used,
they just have to be unsprayed. See what your neighbors have in their
gardens (but ask, first!).

SERVES 6 as a side dish
1¼ cups couscous
1¼ cups boiling chicken stock or water, plus more if needed
2 tablespoons olive oil
1 small garlic clove, crushed
finely grated zest and juice of 1 unwaxed lemon
3 tablespoons extra virgin olive oil
salt and pepper
3 tablespoons chopped flat-leaf parsley leaves
small handful of torn mint leaves
small handful of purple basil leaves
2 scallions, trimmed and very finely chopped
handful of pea shoots, any coarse stalks removed
edible flowers, either whole or petals, divided

Sprinkle the couscous into a bowl, then pour in the stock or water and the regular olive oil.
Cover with plastic wrap and let stand for 15 minutes. Fork it through every so often to separate
and aerate the grains; it should be fluffy. When the couscous is cool, use your fingers to break
down any little clumps. If it still seems a little dry, add more liquid (no more than 3 tablespoons)
and let it stand for a little longer.

Add the garlic, lemon zest and juice, extra virgin olive oil, and plenty of salt and pepper. Taste
for seasoning. Gently mix in the herbs, scallions, pea shoots, and half the flowers. Place in
a broad serving bowl and scatter with the rest of the flowers to serve.

FISH

salmon & cucumber with miso dressing

I ONLY STARTED TO COOK with miso a few years ago and am now addicted to its strong flavor. There are lots of types, some quite sweet, others as umami-rich as yeast extract. Keep the jar in the fridge once you've opened it and use it within three months. You can make this with tuna, too. Serve it on white or brown rice, or just on its own.

SERVES 2 as a light lunch
5½oz salmon fillet, skinned
4½oz cucumber
1 tablespoon white miso paste
1 tablespoon mirin
1 tablespoon light soy sauce
1 teaspoon rice vinegar
1 tablespoon canola or peanut oil
pinch of superfine sugar or smidgen of honey
2 scallions, trimmed and finely chopped
½ tablespoon pickled ginger, finely sliced
1 teaspoon black or white sesame seeds
micro leaves, such as cress or amaranth, to serve (optional)

Cut the salmon into chubby matchsticks. Halve the cucumber and cut it into matchsticks, too (you don't need to peel it or remove the seeds unless you prefer to).

In a small bowl, mix the miso, mirin, soy sauce, vinegar, and oil with the sugar or honey. Toss the salmon and cucumber with this dressing, the scallions, and ginger and divide between two plates.

Scatter with sesame seeds and micro leaves, if you have them. Serve.

shrimp, fennel & tomato pilaf with mint

A GREAT DISH FOR TWO. Let the pilaf cook, then quickly fry the shrimp at the last minute. You can use dry white wine if you don't have vermouth, but I always keep vermouth, as it never fails to come in handy and it's so brilliant with fish.

SERVES 2

½ cup basmati rice

½ fennel bulb

3 tablespoons olive oil

½ onion, minced

1 garlic clove, minced

good pinch of chili flakes

1 cup seeded and coarsely chopped
  well flavored plum tomatoes

½ cup dry vermouth

¾ cup chicken, fish, or vegetable stock

7oz raw jumbo shrimp, shelled and vein removed

salt and pepper

2 tablespoons finely chopped mixed parsley
  and mint leaves

⅓ cup crumbled feta cheese

Put the rice into a sieve and rinse it until the water runs clear.

Halve the fennel and remove the outer layer of leaves—they're usually a little discolored—and the tips, but keep any little fronds. Cut the core out of each piece and discard; chop the flesh.

Heat half the olive oil and sauté the fennel and onion until soft but not colored. Add the garlic and chili flakes and cook for another couple of minutes, then add the tomatoes. Cook for another two minutes. Add the rice and stir gently to combine. Pour in the vermouth and boil until the liquid has reduced by half, then add the stock and return to a boil. Reduce the heat right down and cook for 20 minutes, until the rice is tender and the liquid has been absorbed.

When it's almost ready, heat the rest of the oil in a small skillet and cook the shrimp until they turn pink. Season. Gently fork the herbs and shrimp through the rice and scatter with the feta. Serve immediately.

salmon, fennel & potatoes en papillote with dill butter

THE COOKING TIME will vary depending on the thickness of the fish you use. If you have those chunky fillets (the type most often sold in supermarkets in packs of two or four), the timings here work perfectly. Thinner pieces will cook more quickly. This is good with the crème fraîche sauce on page 133.

SERVES 4

10½oz small round red or
   round white potatoes
½ small fennel bulb
3 tablespoons unsalted butter, melted
8 sprigs of dill, fronds from half of
   them chopped

salt and pepper
4 fillets of salmon (thick center pieces),
   about 5oz each
¼ cup dry white vermouth

Cook the potatoes in boiling water until they are softening, but not completely tender through to the center. Drain and cut into slices about ⅛ inch in thickness.

Trim any little fronds you find on the fennel and reserve. Halve the bulb and remove the outer leaves if discolored or very coarse. Cut out the core from each piece. Cut the fennel into slices (it's best to do this with a mandoline if you have one, but a sharp knife will do).

Preheat the oven to 400°F. Cut out eight rectangles of nonstick parchment paper, each roughly 16 x 15 inches. Two pieces will go together to make each parcel. Set the four double-thickness rectangles of parchment paper on a work surface and brush their middles with butter. Divide the potatoes and fennel between them, layering with the chopped dill and seasoning and drizzling with a little butter as you go. Put the salmon on top, season, and pour on the rest of the butter. Add a splash of vermouth and a whole sprig of dill to each. Carefully pull the doubled baking parchment layers up and over the fish, turning them to seal the edges, but don't roll them up tightly (you want to make a kind of tent). Seal each parcel by twisting the ends up tightly.

Put the parcels on a baking pan and cook for 25 minutes. Unwrap at the table to serve.

bream stuffed with walnuts & pomegranates

SO EASY you can have it midweek (what a treat), but special enough to serve friends at a dinner party, too. Buy the pomegranate seeds if you don't have time to extract them from the fruit yourself. Serve with couscous or grains. Spelt with blackberries, beets, walnuts & buttermilk (see page 112) would be gorgeous alongside, but omit the blackberries.

SERVES 4

4 bream (about ¾lb each), cleaned, trimmed, and scaled

salt and pepper

3 small garlic cloves, minced

1 dried red chile, crumbled

1 cup coarsely chopped walnuts, plus a few more, toasted (see page 112), to serve

¼ cup extra virgin olive oil, plus more to cook and serve

juice of ½ lemon, plus lemon wedges to serve

2 teaspoons pomegranate molasses

2 teaspoons honey

1oz cilantro leaves, finely chopped

½ cup pomegranate seeds, plus more to serve

Preheat the oven to 400°F. Make two diagonal cuts in the flesh of the fish on each side. Season their insides. Mix the rest of the ingredients together and season. Put this mixture inside each fish and lay them in a lightly oiled roasting pan, or in two separate oiled roasting pans. Season the outside of the fish and drizzle with olive oil.

Cook in the oven for 20 minutes, then check the fish at their thickest parts. The flesh should be white, not glassy. If they aren't yet ready, return them to the oven for another four minutes or so.

Scatter with toasted walnuts and pomegranate seeds, drizzle with olive oil, and serve immediately with lemon wedges.

cod with a crab & herb crust

YOU NEED PIECES OF COD all the same size for this, so they're perfectly cooked together. It's best with chunky fillets, rather than thinner pieces (the cooking time here is for thicker ones). You don't have to do the sauce— it can feel like a hassle when you haven't got much time—but it makes the dish a little more special if you're serving it to friends on the weekend.

SERVES 6

For the cod
olive oil, for the roasting pan
6 x 5½oz thick fillets of cod
salt and pepper
10½oz white crab meat, picked over
2 cups fresh white bread crumbs
finely grated zest and juice of 1 unwaxed lemon,
    plus lemon wedges to serve
⅔ stick unsalted butter, melted
leaves from 4 sprigs of tarragon, chopped
2 tablespoons finely snipped chives
½ tablespoon finely chopped parsley leaves

For the sauce
½ cup crème fraîche
2 tablespoons mayonnaise
1 cup watercress leaves, coarse stalks removed,
    chopped
1 shallot, minced
½ teaspoon Dijon mustard
1 tablespoon capers, rinsed of salt or brine,
    chopped
squeeze of lemon juice

Preheat the oven to 400°F. Lightly oil a roasting pan. Put the fillets into it and season them. Mix all the other ingredients together, season, and divide between the fillets, patting the mixture gently down on top of each piece.

Mix together everything for the sauce and season well.

Cook the fish in the oven for 14 to 15 minutes. Serve with the sauce and lemon wedges, with green beans, boiled round red or round white potatoes, and a green vegetable or watercress salad on the side.

deviled mackerel with watercress yogurt

BROILERS VARY A LOT and this cooking time works for my broiler, which does get very hot. You might have to increase the time, but be careful not to burn the fish skin. Instead, move the broiler pan away from the heating element if you have to.

SERVES 6

6 whole mackerel, cleaned and trimmed, about 9¾oz each

1 stick unsalted butter, softened

2 teaspoons cayenne pepper

1 teaspoon ground ginger

½ teaspoon chili flakes

2 teaspoons ground coriander

3 teaspoons superfine sugar

2 teaspoons English mustard

3 teaspoons red wine vinegar

good squeeze of lemon juice

salt and pepper

1¼ cups Greek yogurt

½ cucumber, peeled, halved, seeded, and chopped

handful of watercress, coarse stalks discarded, chopped

Preheat the broiler to its highest setting. Make three slashes in each of the mackerel on both sides. Mix the butter with the spices, sugar, mustard, vinegar, and lemon juice (it works best to just mash it with a fork). Season. Rub this all over the mackerel, inside and out.

Place the mackerel on a broiler rack covered with foil (this makes for easier cleaning) and broil for four minutes on each side, or until cooked through. Mix the yogurt with the cucumber, watercress, and seasoning. Serve the yogurt with the mackerel.

miso & soy glazed mackerel

IF YOU CAN'T BUY really fresh mackerel for this—from a good fish dealer—then make something else. Mackerel deteriorates more quickly than any other fish I know of. This is very simple and, as long as you have the ingredients, easy to put together. Use sriracha or another chile sauce in the glaze if you don't have fresh chiles. Serve with boiled rice and stir-fried greens.

SERVES 4

2 tablespoons sake

2 tablespoons mirin

2 tablespoons white miso paste

1 tablespoon superfine sugar

1 tablespoon soy sauce

2 red chiles, seeded and finely chopped

2 small garlic cloves, crushed

2 teaspoons peeled and finely grated ginger root

4 mackerel fillets

2 scallions, trimmed and chopped diagonally

sesame seeds, to serve

Mix all the ingredients—except the fish, scallions, and sesame seeds—in a shallow dish. Add the fish and turn it over to coat. Cover and refrigerate for at least one and up to six hours.

Preheat the broiler. Remove the fish from the marinade and put it on a foil-lined baking pan (or broiler pan; the foil just makes it easier to clean later). Position the fish about 6 inches from the heat source and cook until just opaque in the center, about six minutes, then transfer to warm plates. Scatter with the scallions and sesame seeds and serve.

trofie with zucchini, shrimp & chili

SIMPLE, QUICK, AND BIG ON FLAVOR. And it's one of those dishes (I think it's the shrimp and vermouth) that makes you feel as if you're eating it on vacation. It's important to cook the zucchini until they are lovely and golden because that's what will transform quite ordinary ingredients into a really good meal.

SERVES 2

5oz trofie or casarecce, or any other pasta shape
salt and pepper
3 tablespoons extra virgin olive oil, divided
9oz zucchini, cut into little cubes
1 garlic clove, crushed
5½oz raw jumbo shrimp, shelled and vein removed
good pinch of chili flakes
¼ cup dry white vermouth (or white wine will do)
juice of ½ small lemon
1 tablespoon chopped dill fronds, or a handful of torn basil leaves

Put the pasta to cook in plenty of boiling lightly salted water until al dente, usually a couple of minutes less than suggested on the package.

Meanwhile, heat 2 tablespoons of the olive oil in a skillet and quickly sauté the zucchini until they're golden all over and quite soft. Add the garlic, shrimp, chili flakes, and seasoning and cook for another minute over fairly high heat, tossing the shrimp around. They will turn pink. Splash in the vermouth and let it bubble away to almost nothing.

Quickly drain the pasta and add it to the skillet along with the lemon juice and whichever herb you're using. Check for seasoning, add the remaining tablespoon of olive oil, and serve immediately. It's not usual—in Italy, at least—to serve grated cheese with seafood (and the dish really doesn't need it), but do so if you want.

seared tuna with preserved lemon, olives & avocado

THIS CAME ABOUT ACCIDENTALLY. I'd made the relish—without
the avocado or the lemon—to go with lamb, then used the leftovers with
a halved avocado that was lurking in the fridge. Once I'd added slivers
of preserved lemon, the combination was perfect. You can use cilantro
or mint instead of parsley, if you prefer.

SERVES 2

For the fish
2 tuna loin steaks
a little olive oil
lemon wedges, to serve

For the relish
¾ coarsely chopped black olives
2 red chiles, seeded and very finely sliced
1 tablespoon white balsamic vinegar

juice of ½ lemon
4½ tablespoons extra virgin olive oil
2 tablespoons chopped flat-leaf parsley leaves
1 small garlic clove, grated
1 large avocado, pitted, peeled, and chopped
1 preserved lemon, fleshy parts removed and
   discarded, rind cut into shreds
salt and pepper

Bring the fish to room temperature.

To make the relish, gently mix everything together. You shouldn't do this too far in advance or
it loses its freshness and gets "tired" and a little soft, but let it sit for 15 minutes or so before
serving so that the flavors can meld.

Use a ridged cast-iron grill pan to cook the fish if you have one, otherwise a good skillet. Brush
each piece of tuna with the regular olive oil and season. Heat the pan until really hot, then cook
the tuna for about 1½ minutes each side so that it's still slightly raw in the middle, like a rare steak.

Serve the tuna with generous spoonfuls of the relish alongside and lemon wedges.

portuguese baked hake & potatoes

It doesn't sound as if this dish will work, or that it's authentic (potatoes baked with mayonnaise is pretty odd), but I've loved it ever since I first tasted it. I don't make mayonnaise especially for this—it's supposed to be quick and easy. I've even left the skin on the potatoes when pushed. It's rich, so it needs a side dish to cut through that. I like a Belgian endive salad. Roast tomatoes are good, too.

Serves 6

1lb 7oz round red or round white
   potatoes, peeled
3 tablespoons olive oil, divided
1 large onion, finely sliced
3 garlic cloves, minced

2 tablespoons finely chopped parsley leaves
salt and pepper
6 hake fillets, about 5½oz each, skinned
juice of ½ lemon
1 cup mayonnaise

Boil the potatoes until tender on the outside, but with a little firmness in the middle. Drain.

Heat 1 tablespoon of the olive oil in a skillet and sauté the onion over medium heat until soft and pale gold (10 to 12 minutes). Add the garlic and cook gently for another two minutes. Stir in the parsley and season. Preheat the oven to 350°F. Put the fish in a gratin dish and squeeze the lemon juice over. Season, then spoon the onion mixture on top.

Slice the potatoes—a little thicker than ⅛ inch—and heat the remaining 2 tablespoons of olive oil in the skillet. Sauté the potatoes (in batches if they don't all fit), seasoning as you do so. You just want to get a little color on them. Don't worry at all if they break up. It doesn't matter.

Spoon the potatoes onto the fish and onions, then spread the mayonnaise on top. It doesn't have to be thick or even as this is a very forgiving dish.

Bake in the oven for 20 minutes, or until the potato topping is golden. Serve immediately.

salmon with tomatoes, pea & basil purée

THIS COULDN'T BE SIMPLER, but it looks very special. If you don't want the hassle of making the tomato sauce, roast some cherry tomatoes on the vine and serve them on the side instead.

SERVES 4

For the purée
1⅔ cups frozen peas
2 tablespoons unsalted butter
3 tablespoons heavy cream
salt and pepper
1oz basil leaves
good squeeze of lemon juice

For the salmon
½ cup extra virgin olive oil (preferably a fruity sort from
    Provence, rather than a grassy Tuscan type)
1 fat garlic clove, skin left on
12 basil leaves, divided
2 plum tomatoes, seeded and chopped
2 tablespoons olive oil
4 x 6oz fillets of salmon

Start with the purée. Cook the peas in boiling water until tender, then drain, reserving the cooking water. Add the butter and let it melt, then tip into a blender or food processor. Add the cream, seasoning, basil, and lemon juice and blend until smooth, pouring in some pea cooking water to get the consistency you want. (You can make this ahead and reheat it at the last minute.)

Put the extra virgin olive oil in a skillet with the garlic (bash the clove with a rolling pin, but leave the skin on) and heat gently. Take off the heat, add six torn leaves of the basil and a good pinch of salt. Let stand for 30 minutes so the flavors can infuse, then remove the basil and garlic. Add the tomatoes. Tear the remaining six basil leaves and add them too, then season.

Heat the regular olive oil in another skillet. Season the salmon on both sides and cook over medium heat, flesh-side down first, for 90 seconds to two minutes, or until golden. Turn and cook on the other side for the same time. Reduce the heat, cover, and cook until it is cooked through but still moist. (How long this takes depends on the thickness of the salmon.)

Quickly reheat the purée while the salmon is cooking. Serve the salmon with the purée and spoon the tomato mixture over the top.

baked sea bass with baby leeks, potatoes, raki & dill

A LARGE WHOLE BASS is impressive but, if you end up having to use smaller fish, remember to reduce the cooking time accordingly, as suggested in the recipe.

SERVES 6

1lb 2oz round red or round white potatoes, cut into ⅛-inch thick pieces

finely grated zest of 1 unwaxed lemon

fronds from a generous bunch of dill, very coarsely chopped, divided

salt and pepper

extra virgin olive oil

1 large sea bass (about 5½lb) or 2 smaller sea bass (each about 2lb 10oz), cleaned, trimmed, and scaled

3½fl oz raki, or Pernod

¾lb baby leeks

Preheat the oven to 400°F.

Spread the potatoes out in a roasting pan with the lemon zest and half the dill. Season and add 2 tablespoons of the oil. Turn everything over with your hands.

Make three slashes on each side of the fish. Rub with more olive oil, push more dill down into each slit, and season inside and out. Place on the bed of potatoes and put some dill into the belly of the fish, too. Pour on the raki.

Cook for 30 minutes for a large fish, or 20 minutes for smaller fish. (If using smaller fish, cook the potatoes on their own for 10 minutes before adding the fish.) Check it is ready: the flesh near the bone in the thickest part of the fish should be white, and not at all "glassy." If it is not yet ready, give it five minutes more. About five minutes before you expect the fish to be ready, steam or microwave the baby leeks until tender. Drizzle them with oil and season.

Move the fish and potatoes carefully to a warm platter. Arrange the leeks around and serve. Roast tomatoes are good on the side.

pugliese fish tiella

THIS—A LAYERED BAKED DISH of potatoes, pecorino cheese, risotto rice, and fish—is usually made with mussels, but I can't be bothered to prepare those during the working week. It's a dish I love, though (how could you not like double carbs baked with pecorino?), so I started to make it with fillets of fish instead. It's pretty miraculous. Stick the whole dish in the oven and just wait for it to be transformed.

SERVES 6
extra virgin olive oil
1 large onion, finely sliced
salt and pepper
1¼lb round red or round white potatoes (no need to peel them; I don't)
14oz can of crushed tomatoes
2 tablespoons chopped flat-leaf parsley leaves
2 garlic cloves, minced
¾ cup finely grated pecorino cheese (Parmesan if you prefer, but I like pecorino here)
¾ cup arborio rice
4 good-sized fillets of white fish (such as cod, hake, or haddock)
1¼ cups fish stock or water

Preheat the oven to 375°F.

Drizzle some oil into a stove-to-oven pan—or a sauté pan that can be used in the oven—and 10 to 12 inches in diameter. Spread the onion out in the pan, seasoning and drizzling with oil.

Either slice or use a mandoline to cut the potatoes really finely. Spread half of these over the onions, then spoon on half the tomatoes, the parsley, half the garlic, and half the pecorino cheese; season and drizzle with oil as you go. Add the rice and lay the fish on top. Put in the remaining potatoes, garlic, cheese, and tomatoes, in that order. Drizzle on a final bit of oil and pour in the stock or water.

Bring to a boil on the stove, then immediately transfer to the oven. Bake for 45 minutes, then check: the potatoes and rice should be tender. If they're not, return to the oven and bake for a little longer. Serve straight from the dish.

smoked haddock with a sharp cheddar crust

A LOVELY AUTUMNAL SUPPER. A salad of baby spinach—with a good mustardy dressing—is delicious on the side.

SERVES 2

⅓ cup white bread crumbs

¼ cup grated sharp Cheddar cheese

½ tablespoon finely chopped parsley leaves

1 tablespoon olive oil

about 1 tablespoon unsalted butter, melted, plus more for the dish

pepper

2 fillets of smoked haddock, about 6oz each

Preheat the oven to 425°F.

Mix the bread crumbs, cheese, and parsley in a small bowl. Add the oil, melted butter, and pepper and mix together.

Arrrange the fish in a buttered gratin dish where it can lie in a single layer. Pat the bread-crumb crust all over the fish.

Cook for 11 to 15 minutes (thicker fish fillets will take longer to cook). Check, by poking into the center of the fish with the tip of a knife, to see whether the fish is cooked right through: cooked fish will have lost that "glassy" look.

Serve immediately. This is also really good with a purée of peas (just blend cooked frozen peas with a little chicken stock and a bit of cream or butter in a food processor). The sweetness of the peas is lovely against the saltiness of the fish.

stir-fried squid with ginger & shaoxing wine

IT'S NOW EASIER to find squid than it used to be. You'll get better stuff at your fish dealer—and they'll prepare it for you—but even supermarket fish counters sell squid whole rather than in those unappetizing-looking rings. And it cooks so quickly. Use sherry if you don't have Shaoxing wine.

SERVES 4

2lb cleaned squid, cut into broad strips
2 lemongrass stalks
1 tablespoon peanut oil
2 garlic cloves, minced
¾-inch piece ginger root, peeled and sliced into very fine matchsticks
2 to 3 red chiles, seeded and finely chopped
4 scallions, chopped diagonally
1 teaspoon palm sugar, or superfine sugar
salt and pepper
1½ tablespoons Shaoxing wine

Pat the squid dry using paper towels, otherwise it doesn't fry very well. Remove the tips and coarser outer leaves from the lemongrass and very finely chop the softer inner core.

Heat the oil in a wok and cook the garlic, ginger, chiles, and lemongrass for one minute over low heat (the garlic shouldn't even color). Whack the heat up high, add the squid, and cook for one minute, then add the scallions, sugar, salt, pepper, and wine and cook for another minute. The wine should bubble away to practically nothing. Serve immediately.

simple goan fish curry

I KNOW, I KNOW, Indian dishes can have a long list of ingredients.
But the hardest thing here is getting the spices out of the cupboard.
After that it's a doddle, even on busy nights.

SERVES 4

4 teaspoons coriander seeds

1 teaspoon cumin seeds

4 dried red Kashmiri chiles

¾-inch piece ginger root, peeled and finely grated

4 garlic cloves, crushed

1 teaspoon ground turmeric

salt and pepper

2 tablespoons sunflower or canola oil

1 onion, minced

1 large plum tomato, diced

14oz can of coconut milk

1 tablespoon palm sugar, or soft light brown sugar

2 teaspoons tamarind paste

1 green chile, seeded and finely sliced

1lb 2oz firm white fish fillets, skinned, cut into 1¼-inch chunks

2 tablespoons chopped cilantro leaves

Toast the coriander and cumin seeds and dried chiles in a dry skillet for about a minute. Crush in a mortar and pestle, then mix in the ginger, garlic, turmeric, and 1 teaspoon of salt.

Heat the oil in a sauté pan over medium heat and fry the onion until soft and golden. Stir in the spice mix. Cook for a couple of minutes, then add the tomato and cook until it is soft. Add the coconut milk, sugar, tamarind, and green chile and bring to just under a boil. Immediately reduce the heat and simmer for about five minutes, until slightly thickened. Taste for seasoning.

Season the fish all over, then add it to the sauce and simmer gently for about four minutes until cooked through. Check again for seasoning. Add the cilantro leaves and serve with rice.

smoked mackerel with potatoes, eggs & dill pickles

SMOKED MACKEREL makes a really easy supper, but you need to start with good fish for a truly excellent meal. Supermarket offerings vary a lot in quality. I get mine from the fish dealer, if I can. Good smoked mackerel is soft and golden, not firm and dark in color.

SERVES 4

10½oz small round red or round white potatoes (no need to peel)

4 eggs

1½ tablespoons extra virgin olive oil (fruity, not grassy)

good squeeze of lemon juice

1 shallot, finely sliced

⅓ cup sweet pickled cucumber, sliced or chopped

fronds from a small bunch of dill, chopped, divided

salt and pepper

⅓ cup mayonnaise

¼ cup buttermilk

4 fillets of smoked mackerel

Cook the potatoes in boiling water until tender, then drain. Hard-boil the eggs (cook them in boiling water for seven minutes), then put them in cold water. Halve, quarter, or slice the potatoes and put them in a bowl with the olive oil, lemon juice, shallot, pickled cucumber, half the dill, and some seasoning. Separately mix together the mayonnaise and buttermilk.

Peel the eggs while they are still warm, quarter them, put them on top of the potatoes, and spoon half the buttermilk dressing over everything. Scatter with some more dill and add the rest to the remaining dressing. Serve the extra dressing with the salad. Put the smoked mackerel fillets on top, either in one piece or in large flakes.

a bit on the side: sauces and relishes

Mostly we think about food in terms of "blocks": a plate of roast vegetables; a seared fish steak; a few grilled chops. The question is how, *easily*, to make those blocks special. Simple accessories, delicious "bits on the side"—butters, relishes, and sauces—help you to make them into a meal.

PINE NUT & ANCHOVY CREAM
Good with roast vegetables, purple sprouting broccoli, drizzled on kale, or roast or grilled chicken or lamb. Add a 1¾oz can of anchovies in oil, ½ cup toasted pine nuts and, 1 crushed garlic clove to a food processor. Blend, then add ½ cup extra virgin olive oil and the juice of ½ lemon. Season with pepper; stir in a few tablespoons of finely chopped parsley.

HERB, CAPER & SHALLOT CRÈME FRAÎCHE
A kind of béarnaise substitute (as long as you get tarragon in there). Serve with hard-boiled eggs, poached chicken, roast salmon, lamb, and steak. To 1 cup crème fraîche add the chopped leaves from 2 sprigs of tarragon, some finely chopped parsley and chives, 2 tablespoons rinsed capers, 1 chopped shallot, 1 tablespoon extra virgin olive oil, and lemon juice, to taste.

ANCHOVY & ROSEMARY SAUCE
Great with fish (bass, bream, mullet, or tuna), roast lamb, bitter leaves such as endive, or beans. Pound 1 teaspoon rosemary leaves in a mortar with 6 chopped anchovies to a coarse paste. Add the juice of ½ lemon, then gradually add 2½ tablespoons extra virgin olive oil and some pepper.

COCONUT & CILANTRO RELISH
This brings a taste of India to roast chicken or fish, or roast cauliflower and carrots. I can eat it straight, by the spoonful. Blend ½ teaspoon toasted cumin seeds, scant 1oz cilantro leaves, 1¾oz grated creamed coconut from a block, 1 seeded green chile, 1 chopped garlic clove, the finely grated zest and juice of 1 lime, salt, and 1½ teaspoon superfine sugar to a purée in a food processor and taste. Chill.

SPICED HERB YOGURT

Toast ½ teaspoon each cumin and coriander seeds in a dry skillet. Crush coarsely. Finely chop ¼oz cilantro leaves and the leaves from 10 sprigs of mint. Stir into 1 cup Greek yogurt with the juice of ½ lemon, ¼ cup extra virgin olive oil, and 3 tablespoons of water. Lovely with roast or grilled lamb, chicken, or pork.

PISTACHIO & FETA PESTO

Put 2½ tablespoons each of pistachio nuts and toasted pumpkin seeds, a 2¼oz bunch of cilantro, 2 chopped garlic cloves, the juice of 2 limes, 1 seeded green chile, and seasoning into a food processor. Blend, adding ½ cup extra virgin olive oil. Stir in ⅓ cup finely crumbled feta cheese and taste for seasoning. Good on grilled chicken or lamb, or roast pumpkin.

MOJO VERDE

A sauce from the Canary Islands that is great on anything grilled, such as lamb, pork, or chicken. Put the leaves from a small bunch each of parsley and cilantro and ¼oz sprigs of mint into a food processor. Add 1 chopped garlic clove, 1 seeded green chile, 1½ teaspoons ground cumin, and 3 tablespoons red wine vinegar. Blend briefly, adding ½ cup extra virgin olive oil. Season and taste.

GREEN TAHINI

For lamb and roast vegetables. In a food processor, place ½ cup tahini, 2 tablespoons plain yogurt, 2 crushed garlic cloves, juice of 1 lemon, ⅓ cup extra virgin olive oil, ½ cup water, and ½oz parsley or cilantro, or a mixture of the two. Season. Blend until you have a sauce as thick as heavy cream; you may need to add more water. Taste for seasoning.

PARSLEY, TOMATO & POMEGRANATE

Seed and finely chop 5oz tomatoes. Toss with lots of finely chopped parsley leaves, minced red onion, 1 crushed garlic clove, a squeeze of lemon juice, ¼ cup extra virgin olive oil, and 1 tablespoon pomegranate molasses. Good with fish, lamb, or avocado.

MINT, ALMOND & HONEY PESTO

Perfect for lamb or on grilled halloumi cheese. Put ½ cup toasted almonds, 3 garlic cloves, 2¾oz mint leaves, 1½oz parsley leaves, 3 teaspoons honey, and the juice of 1 lemon into a food processor. Season. Blend to a purée, adding 1¼ cups extra virgin olive oil in a steady stream.

HAZELNUT PICADA

A Spanish embellishment for roast or grilled pork, lamb, or chicken, or roast cauliflower. Fry 10oz sourdough bread in olive oil until golden. Toast ⅓ cup hazelnuts. Crush both in a mortar and pestle with a clove of garlic. Mix in ½ cup extra virgin olive oil, the grated zest of ½ orange, 1 tablespoon sherry vinegar, 1 tablespoon sherry, and 2 tablespoons chopped parsley.

PRESERVED LEMON & RAISIN RELISH

Serve with lamb, tuna, and as part of a mezze spread. Crush (in a mortar and pestle, or a food processor using the pulse button) 2½ tablespoons blanched almonds, 2 seeded red chiles, 1 teaspoon grated peeled ginger root, 2 small garlic cloves, and ¼oz cilantro with the juice of ½ lemon, 1 tablespoon white balsamic vinegar, and ½ cup extra virgin olive oil. Stir in the chopped rind of 2 preserved lemon and ⅓ cup raisins that have been soaked for a few minutes and then drained. Taste for seasoning.

ROASTS

Squab chickens with sherry, raisins & pine nuts

I WISH I HAD A DOLLAR for every time I've cooked this. Special enough to serve to friends but totally hassle-free. Good with couscous, or little olive oil-roasted potatoes.

SERVES 4
½ cup raisins
1¾ cups medium sherry
4 squab chickens
olive oil
salt and pepper
3 tablespoons toasted pine nuts (see page 242)

Preheat the oven to 400°F.

Put the raisins in a small saucepan with half the sherry and bring to a boil. Remove from the heat and let stand to plump up for 30 minutes.

Put the squab chickens in a roasting pan, or a broad shallow ovenproof dish, in which they will fit quite snugly (if there's a lot of room around them, the juices will evaporate). Drizzle some olive oil over each one and season. Roast for 45 minutes. After 20 minutes, add the remaining sherry.

When there are 15 minutes left before the end of cooking time, add the raisins and the sherry they have soaked in.

After 45 minutes, check for doneness: the birds should still be moist but the juices that run, when pierced between the leg and the rest of the body, should be clear (if there's any trace of pink, cook for a few minutes more, then check again). Serve the squab chickens in the dish in which they've been cooked, or transfer to a warm serving dish and spoon the cooking juices and raisins around. Scatter with the pine nuts.

roast citrus, ginger & honey chicken

ONE OF MY family's favorite meals (and they're fussy). It's very simple to make but looks pretty spectacular, as the chicken turns dark and glossy because of the honey and the orange wedges become nicely caramelized at the edges. If your chicken is getting too dark as it cooks, cover it with foil.

SERVES 6

For the chicken
4lb chicken
1 cup orange juice
¼ cup honey
1½ tablespoons hot sauce, or to taste
3 garlic cloves, grated
1-inch piece ginger root, peeled and grated
finely grated zest of 2 oranges

salt and pepper
1 cup chicken stock or water, if needed

For the roast oranges
4 thin-skinned oranges
olive oil
a little ground ginger
a little soft light brown sugar

Preheat the oven to 375°F. Put the chicken into a roasting pan in which it can lie snugly; if it's too big, the cooking juices around the bird will burn. Whisk the rest of the ingredients for the chicken (except the stock or water) in a pitcher. Pour some of this inside the bird, then pour two-thirds of the rest over it, reserving the remainder. Roast for 45 minutes.

Cut the thin-skinned oranges into wedges and put them into an ovenproof dish where they can lie in a single layer. Sprinkle with olive oil, ground ginger, and seasoning and turn them over in this to coat, then sprinkle the sugar on top. Roast alongside the chicken for one hour.

When the chicken has cooked for 45 minutes, take it out of the oven, scoop up the sticky juices around it with a spoon, and spread them over the skin. Add the rest of the orange juice mixture to the juices in the pan, stirring well to help them blend, then roast for another 45 minutes. Remove from the oven, put on a warm platter, and let the chicken rest for 15 minutes. If the juices seem too thick or intense, add the stock or water to the pan, set it over high heat, and bring to a boil, stirring to dislodge anything stuck to the bottom. Serve in a pitcher. Add the orange wedges to the chicken platter and take it to the table.

roast maple & mustard spatchcock with figs

SPATCHCOCKED CHICKEN—because it's flattened—cooks much more quickly than a whole bird. Supermarkets don't sell them prepared this way, but your butcher will (though it's not hard to do it yourself, as below). Figs, maple syrup, and mustard make a lovely combination. Serve with a grain—brown rice, bulgur wheat, or freekeh—cooked with finely grated orange zest.

SERVES 4

For the chicken
3½lb chicken
2 tablespoons Dijon mustard
¼ cup maple syrup
leaves from 6 sprigs of thyme
salt and pepper

For the figs
8 figs, stalks snipped off, halved lengthwise
2 tablespoons maple syrup
1 tablespoon balsamic vinegar

Preheat the oven to 400°F.

To spatchcock the chicken, place it breast-side down on a cutting board. Using good kitchen scissors, cut through the flesh and bone along both sides of the backbone from the tail end to the neck and remove it. Turn the chicken over and press down hard on the breast until you have flattened the chicken. Remove any big globules of fat and neaten any ragged bits of skin.

Mix the mustard, maple syrup, and thyme leaves. Put the chicken into a roasting pan and brush this all over it, keeping a little back. Season. Roast the chicken for 45 minutes and, 15 minutes before the end of cooking time, spoon the rest of the maple mixture over the chicken.

When there are 10 minutes before the chicken is ready, put the figs into a small ovenproof dish. Mix the maple syrup and vinegar and spoon this over the cut side of each fig. Season and put into the oven with the chicken. The figs will almost caramelize as they cook.

Cut the chicken into pieces and serve on a warm platter with the glossy figs around it.

yogurt-marinated spatchcock with herbs & pomegranates

A YOGURT OR BUTTERMILK marinade does amazing things to chicken, really tenderizing and flavoring it. If you don't have time to marinate this, make something else!

SERVES 4

For the chicken and marinade
3½lb chicken
1 cup plain yogurt (not Greek yogurt)
juice of ½ lemon
3 tablespoons olive oil
4 garlic cloves, crushed
1 teaspoon cayenne pepper

For the dressing
1 small garlic clove, crushed
salt and pepper
1 red chile, seeded and finely chopped
¼ teaspoon ground cumin

1 tablespoon white balsamic vinegar
½ tablespoon runny honey
1 teaspoon pomegranate molasses
1 tablespoon lemon juice
¼ cup extra virgin olive oil

For the salad
2¼oz soft salad leaves
½oz cilantro sprigs (remove some of the
   stalks if they are very long)
½ medium red onion, very finely sliced
seeds from ½ pomegranate
2 tablespoons coarsely chopped pistachios

Spatchcock the chicken (see page 161) or get your butcher to do it. Mix the yogurt, lemon juice, regular olive oil, garlic, and cayenne. Put the bird in a dish where it can lie flat. Make small incisions on the underside and lift the skin of the breast. Pour the marinade over and turn to coat. Cover and put in the fridge. Four hours is good, overnight is even better. Turn a few times.

When you're ready to cook, whisk the dressing ingredients together. Taste for seasoning. Return the chicken to room temperature while you preheat the oven to 400°F.

Lift the chicken out of its marinade, gently shaking off the excess. Put it in a roasting pan, breast-side up, season, and roast for 45 minutes. Toss the salad leaves and cilantro with the onion and dressing. Scatter with the pomegranate seeds and pistachios and serve the chicken—either whole or cut into pieces—with the salad.

roast spatchcock with chiles & smoky migas

THIS IS A FRIDAY or Saturday night dish, as you do have to keep an eye on the migas. Migas are Spanish: bread pieces soaked in milk, then cooked so they are crispy on the outside and fluffy inside. This dish itself didn't originate anywhere except in my head, but is Spanish-inspired.

SERVES 4

3½lb chicken	salt and pepper
½oz cilantro	9¾oz coarse country bread
½oz flat-leaf parsley	¼ cup milk
4 garlic cloves, chopped	½ teaspoon smoked paprika
juice of 2 lemons	1 tablespoon balsamic vinegar
½ cup olive oil, plus 2 tablespoons	1 tablespoon dry sherry
3 red chiles, seeded and finely sliced, divided	4½oz mixed leaves (I like baby spinach and watercress)

Spatchcock the chicken (see page 161), or get your butcher to do it. Put the herbs, garlic, the juice of 1½ lemons, and the ½ cup of olive oil into a food processor. Blend, adding one of the sliced chiles. Put the chicken in a dish where it can lie flat. Make small incisions on the underside. Pour the marinade over, turning to coat. Cover and chill for four hours, if you can. Return to room temperature. Preheat the oven to 400°F. Lift the chicken out of the marinade, put into a roasting pan breast-side up, season, and roast for 45 minutes.

Tear the bread into pieces about the size of closed mussels. Put in a bowl with the milk and ¼ cup of water and toss around with your hands. Let soak for 30 minutes. Gently squeeze the bread. Heat the remaining 2 tablespoons of olive oil in a large skillet and add the bread. Cook over medium heat, turning every so often, until dark golden and crisp. Sprinkle with the paprika and season. Cook a little more, turning; it takes 15 minutes in all.

When the chicken is ready, drain off the juices (there won't be many). Mix them with the vinegar and sherry and add the remaining lemon juice, to taste. Taste; it's a dressing to cover everything so shouldn't be exactly like a vinaigrette, nor too oily. Add the remaining chile slices.

Put the leaves into a large, broad, shallow serving bowl and put the chicken, cut into pieces, on top. Scatter with the migas, then pour the dressing evenly over everything. Serve immediately.

ishita's chicken masala

TWITTER IS A GREAT PLACE for swapping recipes and I like to hear what others are cooking. This is from @foodwithmustard, one of my favorite tweeters. She suggests serving it in quite a British way, with potatoes roasted with chile and lemon, and carrots roasted with ginger and cardamom. Hungry yet? The marinating is optional; do it if you have time. To be super-quick, use a ready-made garam masala blend (about 1½ tablespoons) for the spiced butter, instead of separate spices.

SERVES 6

For the marinade and chicken
2 cups plain yogurt
6 fat garlic cloves, crushed
¾-inch ginger root, peeled and grated
½ tablespoon chili powder
1 teaspoon ground turmeric
salt and pepper
4lb chicken

For the spiced butter
1 stick salted butter, slightly soft
1 tablespoon ground coriander
½ tablespoon ground cumin
1 teaspoon chili powder
1 teaspoon ground cinnamon
1 teaspoon ground cloves
½ teaspoon ground turmeric
2 to 3 fat garlic cloves, crushed
½-inch piece ginger root, peeled and grated

Mix all the marinade ingredients and slather this over the chicken and into the cavity as well. Leave overnight in the fridge (though two hours is fine, or cook without marinating). Mash the butter with all its other ingredients and 1 teaspoon freshly ground black pepper. Chill, to firm up.

Remove the chicken from its marinade, wipe off the excess and return to room temperature. Preheat the oven to 400°F. Carefully slip your fingers in between the skin and breasts. Loosen the skin over the legs and thighs, too. Spread the butter under the skin down over the legs, thighs, and breasts. Spread the remaining butter on top and sprinkle with salt.

Cook the chicken for one hour 10 minutes, basting every so often. Check to see that it's cooked: the juices that run when pierced between leg and bird should be clear, with no trace of pink. Cover with a double layer of foil and let rest for 15 minutes, before serving with the juices.

easy like sunday morning

As a teenager I hated the traditional British Sunday lunch. My parents usually called on friends at midday, leaving me to cook the vegetables (the meat—an excellent piece of Irish beef—was already in the oven). I was a good cook, but there was something about the grinding dullness of this task, and the fact that I tried to combine it with homework, that made me willfully incapable of pulling it off. Sunday after Sunday I would let the carrots boil dry, then try to get rid of the smell while prising the burnt batons off the saucepan.

When I was an au pair in France, I went to a Sunday lunch that made me feel as though I was appearing in a Truffaut movie. "That's the way to do it," I thought. My host Agnes lived with her husband and children in a dilapidated farmhouse. The Sunday lunch in question wasn't grand, but the whole thing was pulled off with style and grace. We drank chilled Pineau de Charente and picked at good charcuterie, then sat down at a table dressed with a simple white cloth and ate roast lamb with petits pois à la française and artichoke hearts (I remember my shock at the absence of potatoes). Afterward there was a green salad—using just one kind of lettuce—with a good dressing; one perfect cheese; and poached peaches. What was special about this meal is that it was unremarkable. There was no endless procession of vegetables and desserts, no complicated dishes. It was chic in its simplicity; served on platters and in big serving bowls, it felt generous and inclusive.

It took me years to approach anything like the ideal that Agnes's lunch had set in my imagination. I loved the idea of a laid-back Sunday lunch, but would always make too many dishes or serve enough desserts to put on a small trolley. When I asked my partner's parents to Sunday lunch for the first time, I actually managed to singe my hair while juggling too many pans. I was able to snip the burnt bit off, but the smell rather gave me away.

I don't like rules—I always want to break them—but here are some guidelines for a relaxed Sunday lunch: no appetizer, you're not running a restaurant. Charcuterie, olives, and radishes are as far as you should go. Have ice, decent gin, or some other aperitif, but remember you're not kitting out a bar. Offer no more than two side dishes (one should be easy to make). One dessert is enough. (Though that's hard advice to follow. I always have a fruit dessert—my favorite—and somehow Sunday lunch is a great place for some old-fashioned stodge such as bread-and-butter pudding.) If you can't be bothered to make dessert at all, a bottle of dessert wine is fine, as is cheese, though one big, good cheese is better than four average wedges.

It's difficult to resist the temptation to offer lots of choice. After all, it seems generous. But with Sunday lunch, as with so many things, less is more. Keep it simple.

honeyed pork loin with plum & lavender relish

I COOK THIS A LOT, using different accompaniments depending on the time of year. You can make the relish with fresh apricots or, in fall, use pears or apples with rosemary. It's fabulous with pickled peaches, too. The pork is still ever so slightly pink in the middle when cooked at this temperature and for this length of time, so cook it a little longer if you want to. However, most people overcook pork, so be careful.

SERVES 8

For the relish
1½lb plums, halved and pitted
½ onion, coarsely chopped
pinch of chili flakes
¾-inch piece ginger root, peeled and grated
⅔ cup soft light brown sugar, or to taste
2 tablespoons red wine vinegar
juice of ½ lemon
salt and pepper
2 sprigs of fresh lavender

For the pork
4½lb boneless pork loin (get the butcher to
    remove the skin but leave about ½ inch
    of fat in place)
leaves from 2 sprigs of rosemary, chopped
2 tablespoons Dijon mustard
3½ tablespoons liquid honey
juice of ½ lemon

Put all the ingredients for the relish, except the lavender, in a heavy pan. Bring to a boil, stirring, then reduce the heat. Simmer for 35 minutes, stirring every so often. Once the plums start to fall apart, add the lavender. Taste for balance; you might need more sugar. Let cool.

Make incisions all over the flesh side of the pork and stuff rosemary in them. Season. Mix the mustard, honey, and lemon juice, pour about three-quarters over and into the incisions. Cover and put in the fridge to marinate for a few hours. Return to room temperature before cooking.

Preheat the oven to 425°F. Roll the loin and tie it at intervals with kitchen string. Put into a roasting pan fat-side up, pouring over the marinade from the fridge. Cook for 15 minutes, then reduce the oven temperature to 350°F and cook for one hour, basting every so often. Add the reserved honey mixture 10 minutes before the end of cooking. If the pork gets too dark, cover it with foil. Check it is cooked: the juices should run clear when pierced. Cover with foil, insulate (use dish cloths), and let rest for 15 minutes. Serve hot or warm, with the relish.

spanish spiced pork with sherried onions

I LIKE THE WAY THAT CUMIN—probably my favorite spice—is used in Spanish food. It's part of the Arab legacy and works surprisingly well with sherry, lending an earthy base note to the sweetness.

SERVES 6

3 garlic cloves, crushed

½ tablespoon ground cumin

1 tablespoon paprika

sea salt flakes and pepper

5 sprigs of thyme, divided

⅓ cup extra virgin olive oil

3lb 5oz boned, rolled pasture-raised pork loin, skin off, but a layer of fat left on

5 small red onions, cut into slim crescent moon-shaped slices

1 tablespoon unsalted butter

2 bay leaves

1¼ cups sweet oloroso or cream sherry

3 tablespoons sherry vinegar

Mix the garlic, cumin, paprika, salt, pepper, leaves from three sprigs of thyme, and the oil. Open the loin so the meaty part is facing you and make incisions all over it. Spread the spice mixture over it and into the incisions. Cover with plastic wrap and let marinate for a few hours in the fridge.

When you're ready to cook, preheat the oven to 300°F and return the meat to room temperature. Roll the pork and tie it at intervals with kitchen string. Heat a stove-to-oven pan with a lid that will fit the pork. Brown the pork all over—the oil from the marinade will be enough—then remove it. Sauté the onions in the oil in the pan until beginning to soften, then add the butter (for flavor), reduce the heat, and cook for four minutes. Add the rest of the thyme, the bay, sherry, and vinegar. Bring to a boil, then reduce the heat. Return the pork and cover. Cook in the oven for one hour 30 minutes, or until cooked but not dry, turning the pork from time to time and basting with its liquid. Remove the pork to a warm dish and let rest for 10 minutes, covered loosely with foil.

Boil the onion mixture until it has thickened a little. Taste and adjust the seasoning if you need to. Serve the pork with the onions, little olive oil-roasted potatoes, and spinach.

slow-cooked pork with chipotle tomato sauce

OK, NOT ONE FOR a Wednesday night. In fact I know that cooking anything for 10 hours might seem like a hassle, but trust me, this couldn't be less demanding. Get it going on a Saturday morning, then serve to friends for a laid-back Saturday supper. It's lovely with hot sweet potatoes (see page 186). If you can't find chipotle chiles in adobo (it comes in cans), just use chipotle chiles soaked in hot water, or chipotle paste.

SERVES ABOUT 10

For the pork
9lb pork shoulder roast, bone in,
  skin removed
1/3 cup Dijon mustard
2½ tablespoons soft light brown sugar
¾ tablespoon sea salt flakes
1 tablespoon paprika

For the sauce
2 tablespoons olive oil
2 onions, minced
6 garlic cloves, chopped
2 tablespoons chipotle chiles in adobo sauce
2 x 14oz cans of cherry tomatoes in thick juice
1½ tablespoons soft dark brown sugar
salt and pepper

Preheat the oven to 225°F.

If the meat seems a little wet, dry it with paper towels. Spread the mustard over the fat. Mix together the sugar, salt, and paprika and pat that onto the mustard. Set the meat fat-side up on a rack in a roasting pan and cook for 10 hours, basting the exposed meat every so often during that time. It will become really soft.

To make the sauce, heat the oil in a pan and sauté the onions until soft (about 12 minutes), then add the garlic and cook for another couple of minutes. Add the chipotles, tomatoes, sugar, and seasoning and bring to a boil. Reduce the heat to low and cook uncovered for 20 to 30 minutes, stirring every so often. You should have a thick sauce, but make sure it doesn't taste too intense and add a little water if you've cooked it too far. Serve the pork with the sauce.

pork loin with pumpkin purée & pecorino

THIS IS A DODDLE, and looks very impressive. Get your butcher to remove the skin from the pork but leave about ½ inch of fat in place. The purée can be made earlier in the day and gently reheated to serve.

SERVES 8

For the pork
4½lb boneless pork loin, skin off
6 garlic cloves, sliced
1 tablespoon fennel seeds
1 teaspoon chili flakes
¼ cup olive oil
salt and pepper

For the purée
2lb 10oz butternut squash or
  well flavored pumpkin
olive oil
freshly grated nutmeg
½ cup mascarpone
pecorino cheese, shaved, to serve

Lay the pork on a board, flesh-side up, and make incisions all over it with a sharp knife. Push slivers of garlic into the incisions. Crush the fennel and chili flakes in a mortar and pestle, add the olive oil, season, and rub this all over the flesh, pushing bits down inside the slits. Place in a dish, cover, and put in the fridge overnight, then return it to room temperature before cooking.

Preheat the oven to 425°F. Roll the loin and tie at intervals with kitchen string (not too tight; it should hold its shape, not look like a sausage). Cook for 25 minutes. Reduce the oven temperature to 350°F and cook for one hour, basting now and then. Cut the squash into wedges and remove the seeds. Put the wedges into a roasting pan, drizzle with olive oil, season, and bake alongside the pork until completely tender, about 40 minutes.

Check the pork for doneness; the juices should run clear with no trace of pink when pierced. Cover with foil, insulate (I use dish cloths), and let rest for 15 minutes.

Discard the skin from the squash. Purée with plenty of seasoning, nutmeg, and the mascarpone. Gently heat, then scrape into a warm dish and top with pecorino shavings. Serve with the pork.

balinese roast pork

BASED ON A DISH CALLED *babi guling*, where a whole pig is cooked with the spice paste. A good, simple, different kind of roast.

SERVES 6 TO 8

For the spice paste
2 lemongrass stalks
3 kaffir lime leaves
1 tablespoon ground turmeric
3 shallots (1 if they're long), chopped
3 red or green chiles, seeded, chopped
3 garlic cloves, chopped
small handful of cilantro leaves
½oz piece ginger root, peeled and grated
2 tablespoons coriander seeds, crushed
1 tablespoon black peppercorns, ground

1 tablespoon palm sugar, or soft light
   brown sugar
juice of 1 lime
2 tablespoons flavorless oil,
   such as peanut

For the pork
4lb pork belly
1 tablespoon ground turmeric
2 tablespoons flavorless oil, such as peanut
sea salt flakes

Take the coarse outer leaves off the lemongrass, then chop the white part (discard the rest). Put everything for the spice paste into a food processor and blend to form a purée. Score the pork skin, marking it in parallel lines. Turn the pork over and make big gashes all over the flesh to create small pockets. Rub the paste over this (not on the skin), pushing it into the pockets. Put the pork in a dish, cover with plastic wrap, and let marinate in the fridge for a few hours.

When you're ready to cook, preheat the oven to 425°F. Roll the pork up and tie it at intervals with kitchen string. Place on a rack in roasting pan, with the join underneath. Mix the turmeric and oil together and rub this all over the meat, then sprinkle it with salt flakes. Roast in the oven for 15 minutes. Reduce the oven temperature to 325°F and roast for another hour and 15 minutes, basting occasionally with the juices. Rest, covered with foil, for 10 to 15 minutes. Remove the string and serve with rice and stir-fried greens. Southeast Asian fruit salad with chile and tamarind (see page 41) is great on the side.

slow-cooked lamb with pomegranates & honey

Easy, but rich and exotic, a real feast for a long lazy weekend lunch or dinner. The lamb should be very soft, almost falling apart, but cooking time varies depending on the time of year, so start checking it after four hours.

Serves 6

For the lamb
4½lb bone-in square-cut shoulder of lamb
9 garlic cloves, coarsely chopped
sea salt flakes and pepper
leaves from a small bunch of mint, torn
¼ cup pomegranate molasses
¼ cup liquid honey
¼ cup olive oil
juice from 4 lemons

To serve
1 pomegranate, or 1¼ cups
   pomegranate seeds
leaves from a small bunch of mint, torn
4 garlic cloves, crushed
1¾ cups Greek yogurt
flatbreads or couscous
salad of watercress or spinach,
   coarse stalks removed

Pierce the lamb all over deeply. Crush the garlic to a paste with salt—it acts as an abrasive—in a mortar. Add the other ingredients for the lamb, starting with the mint, and pound some more.

Put the meat on two huge pieces of foil set at right angles in a roasting pan and pull up the sides so none of the marinade will run out. Pour on the marinade, turning the lamb. Cover and put in the fridge for about 12 hours.

Return the meat to room temperature and preheat the oven to 400°F. Pull the foil over the lamb and seal to form a tent. Place in the oven and immediately reduce the oven temperature to 325°F. Cook for four to five hours, basting with the juices every so often. The lamb is cooked when you can pull the meat apart with a fork. (Cooking times vary a lot depending on the age of the meat you are using, so start checking after four hours.)

Mix the pomegranate seeds with the mint, then add the garlic to the yogurt. Shred the lamb at the table and serve with the yogurt, pomegranate, and mint, plus flatbreads or couscous and a salad of watercress and spinach (a green salad tossed with walnuts or hazelnuts would be great).

roast lamb loin
fillets with zhoggiu

A MINI ROAST—using lamb loin fillets—just for two and with a
Sicilian sauce. Be careful not to overcook the meat. Sautéed potatoes are
perfect on the side.

SERVES 2

For the sauce
2½ tablespoons blanched almonds, toasted
pinch of sea salt flakes and pepper
1 garlic clove, coarsely chopped
¼oz flat-leaf parsley leaves
¼oz mint leaves
1 tablespoon white balsamic vinegar
2½ tablespoons extra virgin olive oil
squeeze of lemon juice

For the lamb
2 lamb loin fillets, trimmed
1 tablespoon olive oil

Make the sauce first so that it's all ready, but don't do it more than 30 minutes in advance: the
fresher the better. Crush the nuts coarsely in a mortar and pestle. Add the salt and the garlic
and continue to crush until the garlic has broken down. Add the herbs—in two batches as it
makes it easier to deal with—and pound hard until you have something like a coarse purée.
While still pounding, add the vinegar and then a little of the extra virgin olive oil at a time.
Add lemon juice to taste—sometimes just a spritz is enough—and check the seasoning.

Preheat the oven to 400°F.

Sprinkle the lamb with salt and pepper and heat the regular olive oil in a skillet over high
heat. Brown the lamb all over to get a good color, then transfer to a roasting pan. Season with
salt and roast for 10 minutes. Cover and keep warm while the meat rests for 10 minutes.

Cut the lamb into neat slices and serve on warm plates. Spoon the sauce alongside and serve,
with sprigs of watercress, if you like.

indian roast leg of lamb

MY VERSION OF A FAMOUS DISH from Lucknow. The marinating
is important in this recipe—it really affects the flavor and texture
of the lamb—so leave it for a whole day if you can. Serve it with rice
and chutneys, or with Indian-spiced roast root vegetables for an
Anglo-Indian dinner party.

SERVES 8

1¼ cups desiccated coconut

3 tablespoons vegetable oil

2 onions, finely sliced

1oz piece ginger root, peeled and finely grated

6 garlic cloves, crushed

seeds from 6 green and 6 black cardamom
pods, ground

2 teaspoons chili powder

2 tablespoons garam masala

⅓ cup cashews

salt and pepper

1½ cups plain yogurt (not Greek yogurt)

juice of 1 lemon or 2 limes

4½lb leg of lamb

Put the coconut in a bowl and pour over just enough boiling water to cover. Let soak for one
hour. Meanwhile, heat the oil and fry the onions until they are deep golden brown; it will take
quite a while. Add the ginger and garlic and cook for another three minutes or so, then add
both types of cardamom and the chili powder and cook for another couple of minutes. Drain
the coconut. Put the onion mixture into a food processor and add everything else except the
lamb. Blend to a purée.

Take the fat off of the lamb and pull off the parchment-like skin, too. Make deep gashes all
over the meat. Put it into a roasting pan and pour over the purée, turning and making sure it
goes into the gashes. Cover with plastic wrap and marinate in the fridge for 24 hours.

When you're ready to cook, preheat the oven to 400°F. Let the lamb return to room
temperature, then cover it with foil and cook for 20 minutes. Reduce the oven temperature
to 350°F and cook for a further 50 minutes, removing the foil for the last 30 minutes so it
browns. Cover the lamb with a double layer of foil and let it rest for 15 to 20 minutes before
serving, with chutneys and yogurt.

roast lamb with peas, onions & vermouth

A ROAST WHERE nearly everything can be cooked in the same dish. Bliss. All you need to add are some little potatoes and maybe roast bell peppers or artichoke hearts tossed with lemon juice and chopped parsley leaves.

SERVES 8
4½lb leg of lamb
3 garlic cloves, cut into slivers
salt and pepper
extra virgin olive oil
1¼ cups dry vermouth
8 small onions, cut into wedges
10 anchovies, drained of oil and chopped
1lb 5oz frozen peas, or fresh peas when in season
leaves from 8 sprigs of mint, coarsely torn

Preheat the oven to 425°F.

Pierce the lamb all over with a small sharp knife to make little incisions. Push all the slivers of garlic into these. Put into a roasting pan and rub all over with salt, pepper, and olive oil. Put into the hot oven and roast for 20 minutes.

Add half the vermouth and all the onions to the pan. Reduce the oven temperature to 350°F. Roast for 15 minutes, basting every so often with the cooking juices.

Pour in the remaining vermouth, add the anchovies, and cook for 25 minutes. Stir in the peas and roast for another 15 minutes. This gives you rosy (but not bloody) lamb.

Move the lamb to a warm platter, cover and leave to rest for 15 minutes. Just before serving reheat the peas and onions, add the mint, and spoon this round the lamb.

lamb with preserved lemon, dates & cumin butter

STUFFED LEG OF LAMB is easy, as long as you have someone around to help you tie the string around it. This isn't a midweek meal, but it's good for friends on a Saturday night, or for Sunday lunch. Serve with couscous, rice, or bulgur wheat. The stuffing and cayenne butter provide enough interest, but a bowl of garlic-scented yogurt would be good on the side (plus maybe an easy vegetable dish).

SERVES 8

For the lamb
6oz kale, coarse stalks removed
1 tablespoon unsalted butter
1 red chile, seeded and chopped
½ teaspoon ground cumin
salt and pepper
5 dates, pitted and chopped
rind of 2 preserved lemons, chopped
4½lb boned leg of lamb

For the butter
½ stick unsalted butter, softened
1 teaspoon ground cumin
1 teaspoon cayenne pepper
3 garlic cloves, grated

Preheat the oven to 425°F. Cook the kale in boiling water for five minutes, then drain and run cold water through it. Squeeze out as much moisture as you can. Chop coarsely.

Melt the butter in a skillet and sauté the kale in this, along with the chile, for a couple of minutes. Add the cumin and cook for another minute. Season and add the dates and preserved lemons.

Lay the lamb on a board, fat-side down, and season. Put the stuffing in the center, then fold the meat over, pressing lightly to seal. Tie at intervals with kitchen string to keep it in shape. Make deep incisions all over with a sharp knife and put it in a roasting pan. Mix all the ingredients for the butter, push into the incisions, and rub all over the outside. Roast, with the join underneath, for 20 minutes. Reduce the oven temperature to 350°F and cook for one hour. Cover with a double layer of foil and let rest for 15 to 20 minutes. Serve with the cooking juices.

CHOPS & SAUSAGES

coffee-brined pork chops with hot sweet potatoes

THIS SOUNDS STRANGE, but it works. The coffee gives the chops a good deep flavor, almost tobacco-ey. Them Southern cooks know a thing or two about pork.

SERVES 4

⅓ cup soft dark brown or muscovado sugar

2 tablespoons sea salt flakes

4 cups freshly brewed hot coffee

4 big pork chops, 9 to 9¾oz each

4 sweet potatoes

pepper

1½ tablespoons rendered pork fat, lard, or flavorless oil

2 tablespoons unsalted butter

leaves from 4 sprigs of thyme

1 red and 1 green chile, seeded and finely sliced

Stir the sugar and salt flakes into the coffee until dissolved. Add 1 cup of cold water and let cool completely. Put this brine in a large container and add the chops, making sure they're submerged. Cover and put in the fridge for six to eight hours.

Remove the chops from the marinade and pat dry with paper towels. Return the chops to the fridge—uncovered, so they dry out a little—for a couple more hours.

When you're ready to eat, preheat the oven to 400°F. Bake the sweet potatoes for about 30 minutes, timing them to be ready at the same time as the chops.

Season the chops (you won't need much salt, but pepper is important), heat the fat or oil in a skillet, and cook over high heat on both sides and on the fat to get a good color. Reduce the heat to medium and continue, turning every so often, until cooked (eight to 10 minutes).

Melt the butter in a small skillet and add the thyme and chiles. Cook for about a minute, then split the sweet potatoes and drizzle the insides with the butter. Serve with the chops.

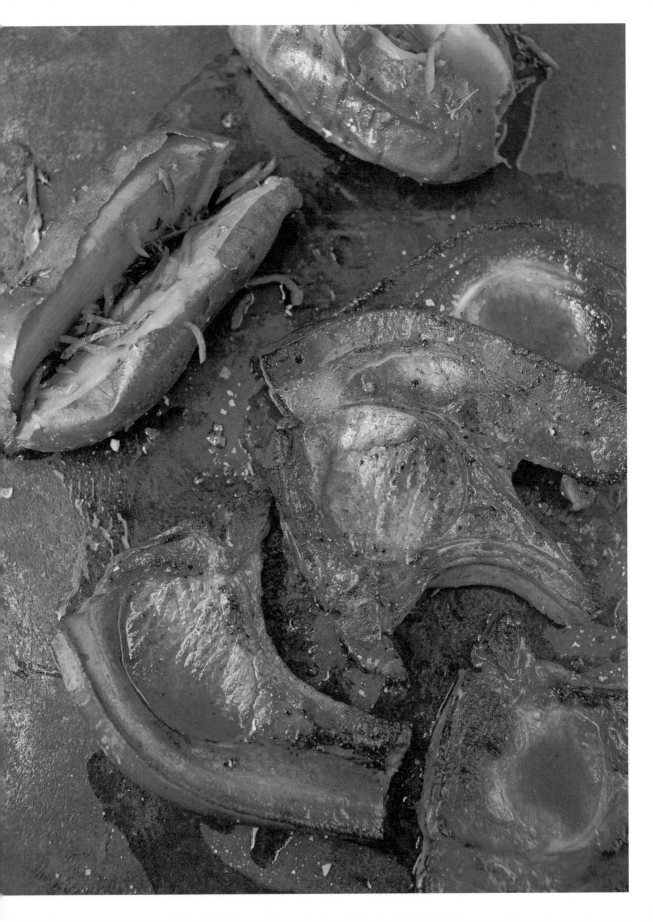

pork chops with mustard & capers

A CLASSIC, but none the worse for that. I love the way the richness of the cream is cut by the capers.

SERVES 4

1 tablespoon olive oil
salt and pepper
4 pork chops, 8 to 9oz each
1¼ cups dry vermouth
1 heavy cream
1½ teaspoons Dijon mustard
2 tablespoons capers, well rinsed of salt or brine

Preheat the oven to 400°F.

Heat the oil in a large ovenproof skillet (or two smaller pans) over high heat. Season the chops all over and cook them for two minutes on each side; you want them good and golden. Now brown the fat, too. Transfer the pan to the oven and cook for 12 minutes.

Wearing good oven mitts and being careful of the hot pan handle, pour the fat out of the pan. Put the chops on a warm plate, and cover to keep warm. Add the vermouth to the pan. Bring to a boil and reduce by half, stirring to pick up all the browned savory bits stuck to the pan, then pour in the cream. Boil until the sauce coats the back of a spoon. Take it off the heat, whisk in the mustard, and add the capers. Taste: it's a strong sauce but it works well with the pork.

Serve the chops with the sauce spooned over the top.

pork chops with figs & marsala

A VERY GOOD SUPPER for two or even four (double the quantities and use two pans). Some people—even Italians—will tell you that dry Marsala doesn't exist. It does. You might have a bit of trouble tracking it down but it's a really useful booze to have around, as it's rich and raisiny. You could also use a medium sherry, if you can't find Marsala.

SERVES 2

2 tablespoons unsalted butter, chilled, divided

2 teaspoons olive oil

5 fat ripe figs, stalks snipped off, halved lengthwise

salt and pepper

2 x 8oz pork chops, boned

1 cup dry Marsala

1 cup well flavored chicken stock

Heat 2 teaspoons of the butter and all the oil in a skillet. Add the figs and cook briefly over high heat on the cut sides, so they get nice and golden. Remove from the pan and set aside.

Season the chops on both sides and quickly brown them in the fat in the pan over medium–high heat. Cook them on both sides and then brown the fat, too. Reduce the heat and continue to cook, turning frequently, until cooked through. Take them out of the pan, set aside, and cover to keep warm.

Pour the fat out of the pan, but don't wipe or wash it. Add the Marsala and bring to a boil, scraping the bottom of the pan. Reduce by about half, then add the stock and reduce that, too, until you are left with enough to make a sauce for two people.

Return the figs to the pan to heat through and soften the uncut sides, then push them to the side and add the rest of the butter. Swirl it around, whisking it into the Marsala and stock. It should make the juices glossy. Serve the chops immediately with the figs and Marsala sauce.

lamb chops with walnut, chile & honey salsa verde

I SEEM TO HAVE GOT INTO pounding things during the last few years. I like highly flavored mixtures such as this salsa verde where the components combine, but keep their identity and texture. This salsa— sweet, sour, and hot—is also good with roast eggplant, and even potatoes.

SERVES 4

1 fat garlic clove, chopped
sea salt flakes and pepper
2 green chiles, seeded and chopped
leaves from a small bunch of mint
½ cup walnuts
1 tablespoon capers, rinsed and coarsely chopped
1 tablespoon honey
juice of ½ lemon
1 cup extra virgin olive oil
8 lamb loin chops
olive oil

Grind the garlic and a pinch of salt to a paste in a mortar; the salt helps as it acts as an abrasive. Add the chiles and mint and pound until you have a coarse mixture. Add the walnuts and pound until you have a coarse purée. Tip in the capers and pound a bit more. Stir in the honey, lemon juice, extra virgin olive oil, and some pepper. Taste to check the sweet-savory balance.

You can fry the chops or cook them on a ridged grill pan. If you're using a skillet, heat a couple of tablespoons of regular olive oil in the pan. If you're griddling, heat a ridged grill pan until really hot and brush the chops with regular olive oil. Either way, season the chops and put them in the skillet or on the grill pan. Cook over high heat until browned on both sides and on the fat, then reduce the heat and cook for a further three minutes each side for chops that are pink and tender in the middle.

Serve the chops with the sauce.

lamb rib chops with hard cider, mint & cream

A GREAT OLD-FASHIONED DISH from Normandy. Lovely in summer (drink it with rosé or cold hard cider), but in fall you can make the same sauce using sprigs of thyme or rosemary (don't use too much, as rosemary is strong) and serve it with either chops or a roast leg of lamb.

SERVES 6

1 tablespoon unsalted butter

2 shallots, minced

generous slug of Calvados or brandy

⅔ cup hard dry cider

leaves from 5 sprigs of mint

1½ cups well flavored lamb stock, or chicken stock will do

salt and pepper

18 lamb rib chops, French trimmed (ask your butcher to do this)

1 cup heavy cream

Get the sauce ready so you can just finish it off when the rib chops are done. Melt the butter in a saucepan and sauté the shallots over medium heat until soft but not colored. Add the Calvados and let it bubble away until there are only a couple of tablespoons left, then add the hard cider with the mint from three of the sprigs and bring to a boil. Boil until reduced by two-thirds. Remove from the heat and let stand to infuse for 30 minutes, then strain and mix with the stock. Return to a boil, then reduce by half. Stir in the cream, season, and bring to a boil. Boil until you have a sauce that just coats the back of a spoon. Set aside.

Heat a ridged grill pan. Season the meat well. When the pan is really hot, cook the rib chops on each side until well colored, pressing the meaty parts down on the grill pan as you're cooking. They should still be pink in the middle, so about a minute and a half on each side should do. Check to see how the rib chops are doing by inserting a sharp knife into one of them.

Quickly reheat the sauce, add the rest of the mint leaves, torn, and check the seasoning. Serve the rib chops on a platter with the sauce and green beans or a watercress salad.

lamb rib chops with fennel & parsley-anchovy relish

OKAY, THIS HAS THREE ELEMENTS—the rib chops, relish, and vegetables—but each is quick to put together. Another time, try the relish and vegetables with baked bream, red mullet, or sea bass instead.

SERVES 6

For the chops and vegetables
2 small fennel bulbs
juice of ½ lemon
14oz round red or round white potatoes
  (no need to peel)
extra virgin olive oil
salt and pepper
12 plum tomatoes, sliced ¼ inch thick
12 lamb rib chops, French trimmed (ask
  your butcher to do this)

For the relish
1¾oz can of cured anchovies, drained of oil and chopped
2½ tablespoons chopped flat-leaf parsley leaves
⅓ cup extra virgin olive oil
juice of ½ lemon

Preheat the oven to 375°F. Quarter the fennel bulbs. Remove the thick outer layer, trim the tops and the bases, and remove the cores. Keep any little fronds. Slice really finely. Put it in a large shallow casserole (I use cast iron, 12 inches across) and toss in the lemon juice. Cut the potatoes in slices ¹⁄₁₆ inch in thickness and toss them with the fennel, 2½ tablespoons of olive oil, and seasoning. Lay the tomatoes on top, season, and drizzle with a little more oil. Bake for 45 minutes, or until you can feel that the potatoes are tender.

To make the relish, just mix the ingredients together, seasoning generously with pepper.

When there are just eight minutes before the vegetables are ready, brush the rib chops with olive oil and season. Cook them in a very hot skillet or ridged grill pan. Start on high heat to get a good color (and brown the fat, too), then reduce the heat and cook until done the way you like them; I prefer them rare. Serve with the vegetables and relish.

chops away

IN THE CAR on the way home from school we knew it was a bad day when mom said, rather grimly, "What do you lot want for supper?" Murmurings of "Dunno" would be followed by the inevitable: "Do you want pork chops?" My siblings and I would exchange oh-God-no glances.

My mom is a really good cook, but pork chops were the dreaded meal, not because of mom's cooking, but because they were so boring. It's not that a high-quality chop—a slab of juicy meat and a bone to chew on—can't make a supremely satisfying supper, it's just that they're one of those basics we turn to when we can't think of anything else. More often than not they end up, unseasoned, under a lukewarm broiler, their only hope of flavor coming from the jar of mustard on the table beside them.

And finding good pork chops isn't easy. Most of us shop in supermarkets for at least some of our food, but you won't find a decent pork chop in any of them. It doesn't matter that they're pasture-raised or that you cook them with the utmost care, if you want good pork chops, go to a really good butcher (or a farm stand or a farmer's market) and buy chops that have been taken from a heritage-breed pig. They won't be cheap, but they're the only pork chops worth bothering with. The meat will be succulent, sweet, even slightly gamey. If you can't afford them, eat something else and have pork chops as a once-in-a-while-treat.

Small chops come from the blade end and are called rib chops. Center cut chops come from the middle loin. Chops that come from the sirloin (or sometimes the extreme shoulder end) are called end chops, and they don't have a bone. I start chops off in a skillet over high heat to get a good color on each side (I also cook the fat by propping the chops up on their sides), then reduce the heat and cook them through, about another four minutes on each side.

As most lamb isn't (yet) intensively farmed, it's a less problematic choice. There are neat little rib chops from the rack, loin chops, which are meatier, then sirloin chops, which are really generous and come from the fat, sirloin end of the lamb's leg and hip section. Lamb chops are a quick option: the meat should be pink so, unlike with pork, you don't have to worry about cooking it all the way through. Some of the best lamb chop meals are incredibly simple, too. I remember the first time I had lamb *scottadito* ("burn your fingers" lamb) in a restaurant in Italy. Tiny lamb cutlets, marinated in olive oil, rosemary, and chile, then grilled with care, arrived on a big platter and we just ate them with our hands. I still think about this dish 25 years later, which says something.

Have a look at my selection of sauces and relishes (see pages 152 to 153) to find ideas for both lamb and pork. Chops aren't a cheap option, so they need to be treated with respect. They should never be the dull default, and they needn't be.

oregano lamb chops with greek htipiti

SERVE THESE MARINATED CHOPS simply with yogurt, if you prefer
(or yogurt with spiced butter poured over, see page 260), or add
some finely chopped chile to the htipiti if you like a little heat.

SERVES 6

For the marinade and chops
3 garlic cloves, crushed
1 tablespoon dried oregano
½ cup olive oil
juice of 2 lemons, plus lemon wedges to serve
salt and pepper
12 lamb loin chops, or rib chops

For the htipiti
1 small red onion, quartered
4 red bell peppers, halved and seeded
3 tablespoons extra virgin olive oil
1 small garlic clove, crushed
1 cup finely crumbled feta cheese
2 tablespoons lemon juice, or to taste

Mix everything for the chops in a large bowl, seasoning well, and add the chops. Turn them over in the flavored oil to coat, cover with plastic wrap, and let marinate in the fridge for a few hours.

When you're ready to cook, return the lamb to room temperature and preheat the oven to 400°F. Brush the onion and bell peppers with a little of the extra virgin olive oil, put them in a roasting pan, season, and roast for 30 minutes, or until completely soft. Either chop them by hand, or blitz very coarsely in a food processor (use the pulse button or you'll end up with a purée), adding the garlic. Stir in the crumbled feta cheese, remaining extra virgin olive oil, and lemon juice, then mash it together and check the seasoning.

Preheat a ridged grill pan until it's really hot. Cook the chops for a couple of minutes on each side—and on the fat, too, to get some color—until they are done to your liking (loin chops take longer). Transfer to a platter and serve with lemon wedges and the htipiti.

spiced lamb rib chops with dates, feta, sumac & tahini

I CANNOT RESIST the combination of lamb, sweet dates, and nutty tahini. You need plenty of herbs, though, to cut through the sweetness here, so use loads and don't stint on the feta cheese either. Greek yogurt and shreds of preserved lemon zest would help, too. Serve with couscous, bulgur wheat, or little olive oil-roasted potatoes.

SERVES 4

8 lamb rib chops, French trimmed
    (ask your butcher to do this)
1/3 cup olive oil
2 teaspoons ground cumin
3 garlic cloves, crushed, divided
1½ teaspoons Aleppo pepper, or
    1 teaspoon cayenne
juice of 1 lemon, divided
1/3 cup extra virgin olive oil, divided

3 tablespoons tahini
¼ cup Greek yogurt
salt and pepper
10 fat, soft dates, pitted and quartered
2/3 cup crumbled barrel-aged feta cheese
leaves from a big bunch of mint, torn if large
fronds from a bunch of dill, very coarsely chopped
baby leaves or micro leaves (whatever you can find)
1 tablespoon white balsamic vinegar
¼ teaspoon sumac

Put the lamb in a shallow container with the regular olive oil, cumin, two of the garlic cloves, the Aleppo pepper, and half the lemon juice. Turn, cover, and chill for 30 minutes to two hours.

Tip the remaining garlic and lemon juice, 3 tablespoons of the extra virgin olive oil, the tahini, yogurt, and seasoning into a blender, pour in 3 tablespoons of water, and blend. It should be the consistency of thick heavy cream, so add more water if you need to, then check the seasoning.

Heat a ridged grill pan or skillet until really hot. Lift the lamb out of the marinade, shaking off excess, and cook over high heat, seasoning as you do, until they are cooked the way you like them. I prefer them rare.

Put the dates, feta cheese, herbs (reserve some to garnish), and leaves onto a platter and toss with seasoning, the vinegar, and the remaining extra virgin olive oil. Put the rib chops on top, drizzle on some of the dressing (serve the rest on the side), garnish with the reserved herbs, and sprinkle with the sumac. Serve immediately.

honeyed sausages with blackberry & caraway slaw

GOOD-QUALITY SAUSAGES are vital here. The slaw is still lovely without blackberries, but cultivated berries are easy to buy in fall, so you don't have to pick your own.

SERVES 4

For the sausages
2 tablespoons wholegrain mustard
⅓ cup honey
salt and pepper
8 good-quality chunky pork sausages

For the slaw
1½ teaspoons caraway seeds
1½ tablespoons maple syrup
1 teaspoon Dijon mustard

1½ tablespoons apple cider vinegar
⅓ cup extra virgin olive oil
2½ cups baby spinach
¼ small red cabbage, core removed, very finely sliced
1 small apple, cored and cut into matchsticks
¼ small red onion, sliced wafer thin
2 tablespoons walnut pieces, toasted (see page 112)
1 crumbled dried chile
½ cup blackberries

Preheat the oven to 410°F.

Mix the wholegrain mustard and honey with some seasoning. Put the sausages into a roasting pan large enough for there to be a little room around them (too big a pan and the juices will boil off and burn; too small and the sausages will sit in a pool of liquid and won't turn lovely and glossy). Pour the honey mixture over the sausages to coat, then roast for 25 to 30 minutes, turning them over every so often. They should look as shiny and dark as chestnuts. If not, cook for a little longer.

Toast the caraway seeds in a dry skillet for 20 seconds, then put onto a plate to cool. Whisk together the maple syrup, Dijon mustard, vinegar, and extra virgin olive oil and add the seeds.

Bunch the spinach leaves on a cutting board and slice them finely. Put into a serving bowl with the other slaw ingredients, pour on the dressing, and gently toss. Serve with the sausages.

simply sausages

PRETTY MUCH EVERYONE loves a sausage. The fact that we often eat them when having a good time—hot dogs at music festivals, BBQs in the backyard, sitting around a campfire—means they come with the happiest associations, too. Give me the most average sausage in a bun with fried onions and mustard and I'll want to kick my shoes off and turn the music up *loud*. When I lived in France for a year, I felt sorry for them. Despite the fact that they have great charcuterie, hot dogs were, apparently, beyond their imagination. (This situation has changed, at least in Paris, where American food trucks have introduced *chiens chauds* served in mini baguettes. Oooh la la.)

We have been told to watch our consumption of sausages—the nitrites and nitrates that go into them (as well as into bacon, ham, and salami)—are not good for you, but I won't be giving them up (I eat them every couple of months). All the more reason that, when you *do* have sausages, you make something good with them.

Not so long ago, here in Britain, sausages were just a cheap and cheerful supper. There wasn't much choice, only pork (fleshy pink and rather unappetizing under plastic wrap) served with mashed potatoes or, once we started to take them more seriously, onion gravy. By the the mid-1990s every gastropub worth its blackboard menu was swimming in onion gravy. Chefs feverishly cooked links of meaty Cumberland sausages and food markets began to boast specialty sausage stands. This enthusiasm has continued and broadened. Spanish chorizo (cured Spanish sausage spiced with paprika) is so popular you'd think we all had an aunt hidden away in Andalucia, though, despite our ardor, we still can't pronounce it: it's chor-*eetho*, amigos, not chor-*itso*. It ain't Italian.

Buying really good (and thus more expensive) sausages less often has made me appreciate them more. While we now cast our net wider in terms of types of sausage, I'll bet you can't think of much to do with them. Don't get me wrong. There's nothing the matter with a plate of sausages and fried eggs. But sausages make fine stews, and gorgeous smoky braises when paired with beans or lentils. Or brown sausages, then cook them in stock with round red or round white potatoes, blood sausage, and onions to make a pot of soothing Dublin Coddle (don't be misled by the simplicity of this, it's really good); or with pears, rosemary, onions, and hard cider. You can go spicy, too, serving hot Italian sausages with braised lentils, or frying them with purple sprouting broccoli, garlic, red chile, and a splash of dry vermouth. Chorizo can be sautéed with red bell peppers and potatoes, stir-fried with squid and cilantro, or just eaten in sizzling slices with a glass of cold fino.

There are good accompaniments, too, and I don't just mean stewed apples: plums can be cooked with red wine vinegar, brown sugar, and ginger; or make a simple sauce of reduced cream, Dijon mustard, and a squeeze of lemon juice. Fried sausages? A hot dog? They'll always make me smile. But they're only the beginning…

spanish rice with chorizo, beans & pumpkin

DISHES MADE WITH SPANISH RICE must, unlike risotto, be left alone: you shouldn't stir them, which is a big plus in my opinion. It means they're easy. The only taxing thing here is cutting the pumpkin into chunks and peeling it. Do try and use a dish about the same size as mine, as using something bigger or smaller will affect the cooking time.

SERVES 6

generous pinch of saffron strands (optional)

1½ tablespoons olive oil

10 to 12 chorizo sausages (the type that need cooking, not the cured version)

1 large onion, coarsely chopped

2 garlic cloves, crushed

14oz sweet pumpkin or squash, peeled, seeded and cut into 1-inch chunks (prepared weight)

1¾ cups coarsely chopped tomatoes

1 tablespoon smoked paprika

1 teaspoon chili flakes (optional)

14oz can of white beans, drained and rinsed

2½ pints chicken stock

1½ cups Spanish paella rice

salt and pepper

2 tablespoons chopped flat-leaf parsley leaves

lemon wedges, to serve

Put the saffron in a pitcher, if using, with 3 tablespoons of just-boiled water. Let stand for 30 minutes.

Heat the oil in a large deep skillet, or a broad shallow cast-iron casserole at least 12 inches in diameter, and brown the sausages. You want to color them on the outside, not cook them through. Remove and set aside.

Sauté the onion and garlic in the same pan over medium heat until soft and golden. Add the pumpkin and tomatoes and cook for four minutes. Stir in the paprika and chili flakes, if using, and cook for a minute, stirring, then tip in the beans and the stock, saffron, and its soaking liquid.

Return the sausages to the pan, bring the stock to a simmer, and cook over very low heat for 10 minutes. Pour the rice around the sausages and season everything well. Cook for 25 minutes, uncovered, but don't stir the rice. When all the stock has been absorbed and the rice is tender, scatter with parsley and serve with lemon wedges.

baked sausages with apples, raisins & hard cider

A GREAT COLD WEATHER SUPPER for very little effort. You don't have to soak the raisins in brandy if you feel you don't deserve it (though I'm sure you do); boiling water is fine.

SERVES 6

⅔ cup raisins

3 tablespoons brandy (apple brandy or regular brandy, or you can use whiskey)

2 large onions, peeled

3 eating apples, quartered and cored

3 tablespoons olive oil

salt and pepper

8 sprigs of thyme

1 tablespoon soft light brown sugar

12 pork sausages

1 cup hard dry cider

Preheat the oven to 375°F.

Put the raisins into a saucepan and add the alcohol. Bring to just under a boil, then take the pan off the heat and let the raisins plump up for 30 minutes. Halve the onions and cut each half into four wedges. Put the onions and apples into an ovenproof dish that will hold the sausages in a single layer (it makes life easier if it's a dish you can also serve from). Add 2 tablespoons of the olive oil, the seasoning, and thyme and toss the apples and onions with your hands. Sprinkle sugar on each wedge of apple. Scatter the raisins and their soaking liquid in among the apples.

Heat the remaining 1 tablespoon of oil in a skillet and fry the sausages until golden all over; you are just doing this for color. Put them on top of the apples and onions and pour in the cider.

Bake for 50 minutes to one hour. The sausages will become dark brown, the apples golden and completely tender, and the liquid should be absorbed by the onions. Serve immediately with mashed potatoes and a green vegetable, such as Savoy cabbage or a watercress salad.

smoked sausage with split pea purée & caraway butter

It's amazing what you can do with a package of split peas. Sometimes I eat the purée here just on its own, with cucumber tossed in sour cream. You could also serve the purée with regular sausages that you've fried, though smoked sausage is easier to get than it used to be.

Serves 4

1¼ cups yellow split peas

1 onion, minced

1 medium carrot, finely chopped

1 leek, white part only, chopped and rinsed

1 teaspoons dried marjoram

salt and pepper

2½ pints mixed stock and water, or just water

1 large smoked sausage, such as Morteau (the usual weight is ¾lb)

generous grating of nutmeg

1 tablespoon white wine vinegar

½ stick unsalted butter

2 teaspoons caraway seeds

Put the split peas into a saucepan with the onion, carrot, leek, marjoram, seasoning, and stock and water, or water. Bring to a boil, reduce the heat to a simmer, and cook for about one hour, or until completely soft and a thick purée. When the split peas still have 40 minutes to go, put the sausage into a separate pan of boiling water. Reduce the heat and poach it for 40 minutes.

Return to the purée: add more seasoning (it needs plenty), the nutmeg, and vinegar and scrape into a warm bowl. Heat the butter in a skillet and add the caraway. Cook over medium heat until you can smell the caraway, but don't let the butter burn, then pour it over the purée.

Slice the sausage and serve with the purée. Warm potatoes tossed with chopped dill pickles, or sliced cucumber mixed with sour cream, are good on the side.

spaghetti with spiced sausage & fennel sauce

EASY, QUICK AND A CROWD PLEASER. My kids love it, and they're pretty picky. Omit the fennel seeds if you don't have any. You can use pasta shapes instead of spaghetti, if you prefer.

SERVES 4

14oz spicy pork sausages, preferably Italian

2 tablespoons olive oil

1 fennel bulb

1 large onion, minced

½ teaspoon chili flakes

pinch of fennel seeds, bashed in a mortar and pestle

2 garlic cloves, crushed

1 cup white or red wine, or dry vermouth

14oz can of cherry tomatoes in thick juice

salt and pepper

2 teaspoons soft light brown sugar

2 tablespoons extra virgin olive oil

10½oz spaghetti

finely grated Parmesan or pecorino cheese, to serve

Remove the sausage casing and form the meat into hazelnut-sized pieces. Heat the regular olive oil in a sauté pan and brown them over high heat until a good color all over. Remove from the pan and set aside.

Halve the fennel bulb and take off the tough outer leaves. Trim the tips—keep any little fronds—and cut each piece in half again. Trim the base of each, discard the core, then finely chop. Sauté with the onion over medium–low heat until soft. Add the chili flakes, fennel seeds, and garlic, plus any fronds, and cook for two minutes. Increase the heat, add the wine, and let it bubble until reduced by half. Add the tomatoes, bring to a boil, then reduce the heat to low. Season really well, add the sugar, and cook for about 20 minutes, uncovered. Now return the sausage and cook for 15 minutes, stirring from time to time. You may need a little water (it depends how much your sauce has reduced). You should have a good thick sauce that will coat the pasta, and not a solid purée. Drizzle in the extra virgin olive oil; it's great for extra flavor and enriches the sauce.

Cook the pasta in plenty of boiling salted water until al dente—usually a couple of minutes less than the package suggests—then drain (not too thoroughly; a little cooking water helps the sauce) and return it to the pan. Stir the sauce into the pasta. Serve with Parmesan or pecorino cheese.

merguez with sweet potatoes, beans & chermoula

THIS IS MOROCCAN INSPIRED; chermoula is a relish that can be used as a sauce or a marinade. Seasoning is important here, as beans are bland without it. It might be a long list of ingredients, but I often make this midweek. It's not taxing; just 15 minutes' work and then into the oven.

SERVES 4

For the sausages
2 tablespoons olive oil
8 merguez sausages
1 large onion, coarsely chopped
1lb 5oz sweet potatoes, in chunks
2 garlic cloves, crushed
2 teaspoons ground cumin
1 teaspoon ground ginger
¼ teaspoon chili flakes
14oz can of cherry tomatoes in thick juice
1 cup chicken stock
14oz can of cannellini or lima beans, drained
14oz can of chickpeas, drained
1 teaspoon soft light brown sugar (optional)

For the chermoula
⅓ cup extra virgin olive oil
½ teaspoon ground cumin
½ teaspoon ground coriander
½ teaspoon sweet paprika
1 red chile, seeded and finely chopped
juice of 1 lemon
1 garlic clove, crushed
½oz cilantro leaves, chopped
2 tablespoons chopped flat-leaf parsley

Preheat the oven to 350°F. Heat the regular oil in a broad shallow cast-iron casserole or ovenproof sauté pan (ideally 12 inches across) and fry the sausages to get a good color. Remove and set aside. Add the onion and sauté over medium heat until golden and soft, about 12 minutes. Add the sweet potatoes and cook for two minutes, then the garlic, cumin, and ginger and cook for another two minutes. Stir in the chili flakes, tomatoes, stock, beans, and chickpeas. Season well. Add the sugar, if using (canned tomatoes need it). Bring to a boil, return the sausages, then cook in the oven for one hour. Stir twice during cooking. The sauce will thicken.

Meanwhile, mix everything for the chermoula together. You can spoon this over the finished dish or offer it in a bowl on the side. A bowl of Greek yogurt is good here, too.

CHICKEN

turkish spiced chicken with parsley salad

THE THING ABOUT TURKISH FOOD is that it's incredibly simple, but full of surprises. We don't think of basing a whole salad on parsley—we regard it as an herb, rather than a salad leaf—but this works brilliantly. Try it with spiced grilled fish or lamb chops, too.

SERVES 4

For the chicken
⅓ cup olive oil
1½ teaspoons ground cumin
1 teaspoon ground allspice
1½ teaspoons Aleppo pepper, or
  1 teaspoon cayenne pepper
4 garlic cloves, crushed
salt and pepper
8 skinless boneless chicken thighs
lemon juice and lemon wedges, to serve

For the salad
5oz tomatoes
very large bunch of parsley, weighing about ¼lb
½ small red onion, minced
1 small garlic clove, crushed
1 tablespoon lemon juice
¼ cup extra virgin olive oil
1 tablespoon pomegranate molasses

Mix the regular olive oil with the spices, garlic, and seasoning. Put the chicken in a dish and pour this over it. Cover and put in the fridge to marinate, from 30 minutes up to four hours.

Halve and seed the tomatoes, then dice the flesh fairly finely (you can skin them too, but I can never be bothered). Chop the parsley leaves finely (use the stalks for something else) and mix with the tomatoes, onion, and remaining salad ingredients.

Heat a ridged grill pan, or a skillet, until very hot. Lift the chicken out of the marinade, shaking off excess, then cook it. Start on high heat to get a good color on both sides, then reduce the heat and cook, turning, for about eight minutes in total, or until cooked through. Squeeze lemon juice all over the chicken and serve with lemon wedges and the salad.

chicken piccata

A SIMPLE CLASSIC. Usually this is made with chicken breasts but you can use thighs, too. It's often served with pasta, either plain or try Orzo with lemon and parsley (see page 100).

SERVES 4

2 thick skinless chicken breasts, or 8 small skinless boneless chicken thighs
2 tablespoons extra virgin olive oil
2 tablespoons unsalted butter, chilled, divided
salt and pepper
¼ cup dry vermouth
2 tablespoons lemon juice
2½ tablespoons capers, rinsed of salt or brine
¼ cup finely chopped parsley leaves

If you're using chicken breasts, cut them in half horizontally with a sharp knife and put them between two sheets of plastic wrap or nonstick parchment paper. Bash them with a meat mallet or a rolling pin until slightly flattened. Thighs just need to be opened out.

Heat the oil and one-third of the butter in a large, heavy skillet. Once the butter has foamed, sauté the chicken breasts for two minutes on each side, seasoning as you go, until they are cooked through. You want a good color on the outside. If you are using thighs, you'll need to cook them for longer. Transfer the chicken to a platter, cover loosely, and keep warm.

Add the vermouth and the lemon juice to the skillet and bring the mixture to a boil. Swirl in the rest of the butter, allowing it to melt, then add the capers and parsley. Check for seasoning: you'll need pepper, but probably not salt. Pour this over the chicken and serve.

orange-oregano roast chicken, olive gremolata

SIMPLE BUT STRIKING to look at. Serve with a watercress salad and little potatoes that you've roasted in olive oil or a rice pilaf.

SERVES 6

For the chicken
12 skin-on bone-in chicken thighs
leaves from 1 bunch of oregano, chopped
8 garlic cloves, crushed
juice of 2 oranges and finely grated zest of 1,
    plus 2 small–medium oranges, preferably
    thin-skinned, cut into thin slices
⅓ cup extra virgin olive oil, divided
sea salt flakes and pepper
a little granulated sugar

For the gremolata
7oz mixed green and black olives, pitted
    and finely chopped
2 garlic cloves, minced
2 red chiles, seeded and finely sliced
zest of 1 orange, removed with a zester
leaves from 2 sprigs of oregano, coarsely chopped
⅓ cup extra virgin olive oil
1 tablespoon orange juice
1 tablespoon white balsamic vinegar
squeeze of lemon juice

Trim the chicken thighs of scraggy bits of skin. Pierce the undersides with a sharp knife and put in a dish. Add the oregano, garlic, orange juice and zest, ¼ cup of oil, and the pepper. Mix with your hands, cover, and put in the fridge for a few hours (overnight is even better). For the gremolata, put the olives, garlic, chiles, zest, and oregano on a board and finely chop them. Put in a bowl with the rest of the gremolata ingredients and set aside to let the flavors infuse.

Preheat the oven to 375°F. Take the chicken out of the marinade, shaking off excess. Heat the remaining oil in a large ovenproof sauté pan or shallow cast-iron casserole in which the chicken can lie in a single layer. Brown the chicken, in batches, on both sides, finishing skin-side up. Scatter with sea salt flakes and roast for 20 minutes.

Lay some of the orange slices under the chicken and the rest on top. Spoon the cooking juices over the oranges, then sprinkle a little sugar over the slices. Roast for another 20 minutes; the chicken and oranges should be cooked. Scatter the gremolata on top. Serve straight from the sauté pan or casserole.

andalusian chicken with honey, saffron & almonds

THIS DISH PRETTY much looks after itself once in the oven. If you don't like saffron, omit it, and the dish will still be very good. A picada is used in Spain to thicken cooking juices and give a final "lift" to dishes. Don't worry, it's not overwhelming because the flavors of the garlic and parsley are softened by the toasted bread.

SERVES 4

For the chicken
generous pinch of saffron strands
1½ tablespoons olive oil
8 skin-on bone-in chicken thighs
salt and pepper
2 onions, chopped
2 garlic cloves, crushed
1½ teaspoons ground ginger
1 cup medium sherry
½ cup chicken stock or water

juice of 1 small lemon, divided
¼ cup liquid honey, divided

For the picada
¼ cup blanched almonds
2 tablespoons finely chopped parsley leaves
1 garlic clove, chopped
½oz fried bread (fried in olive oil),
    broken into chunks
2 tablespoons sherry

Put the saffron in a pitcher and add 3 tablespoons of just-boiled water. Let steep for 30 minutes.

Preheat the oven to 400°F. Heat the oil in a wide, shallow cast-iron casserole (12 inches across) in which the chicken can lie in a single layer. Brown the thighs over medium–high heat; they don't need to cook through. Season as you go. Remove from the pan. Pour off all but 1½ tablespoons of the fat from the pan, put back over medium heat, and cook the onions until golden. Add the garlic and ginger and cook for two minutes, then add the sherry, saffron with its water, and stock, increase the heat, and let it come to a boil. Reduce the heat and add half the lemon juice and honey. Return the chicken, skin-side up, and cook in the oven for 40 minutes. Put everything for the picada, except the sherry, in a mortar. Bash until coarse. Stir in the sherry.

When the dish has cooked for 30 minutes, mix the remaining lemon and honey and brush it onto the chicken. Sprinkle the picada around the chicken and cook for the final 10 minutes.

tim's parmesan chicken

MY FRIEND TIM served this for a load of children and adults one weekend and I immediately pounced on the recipe. Now a staple in my house, it's a throw-it-all-in-the-oven dish, the best type for family cooking. If you're in a rush you can skip the marinating part. Just omit the olive oil and add the minced garlic to the bread-crumb mix instead.

SERVES 4 TO 6

10 good-sized skinless boneless chicken thighs

1½ tablespoons olive oil

4 garlic cloves, minced

salt and pepper

2 cups white bread crumbs

½oz parsley leaves, finely chopped

1 cup finely grated Parmesan cheese

3 large eggs, lightly beaten

Pierce the chicken all over with a sharp knife. Put it in a shallow dish and rub with the olive oil and garlic. Add pepper, cover, and put in the fridge for a few hours if you have the time. If you don't, you can skip this marinating stage (see recipe introduction).

Preheat the oven to 350°F; return the chicken to room temperature (if you've marinated it).

Mix the bread crumbs with the parsley, Parmesan cheese, and seasoning. Put this into one broad, flat dish and the eggs into another. Lift the chicken out of the marinade and season all over. Dip each thigh into the eggs and then into the crumbs. Roll each one up—not tightly, just form it approximately into the shape of a thigh—and place in a shallow ovenproof dish. Scatter with any leftover bread-crumb mixture and pour over the remaining egg.

Cook in the oven for 45 minutes. The top should be golden and the chicken cooked right through. Serve immediately with a green salad and olive oil-roasted potatoes.

moroccan-spiced chicken with dates & eggplant

A USEFUL, NO-HASSLE, chuck-everything-in-together dish. You don't even need to brown the chicken (though make sure you sprinkle the skin with sea salt flakes, to help it crisp up). Find a dish that has about the right dimensions, to ensure that it works well. Don't be afraid of assertive seasoning—rice dishes such as this need it—and don't skip the step where you wash the rice, or it will end up sticky. A bowl of Greek yogurt is good on the side.

SERVES 4 TO 6

1 cup basmati rice

1 large onion, coarsely chopped

1 eggplant, cut into cubes

3 garlic cloves, crushed

1 teaspoon ground ginger

1 tablespoon ground cumin

1½ tablespoons harissa

finely grated zest and juice of 1 orange

8 skin-on bone-in chicken thighs

12 dates, pitted and sliced

2½ cups boiling chicken stock

sea salt flakes and pepper

3 tablespoons olive oil

2 tablespoons chopped pistachios

Preheat the oven to 400°F.

Put the rice into a sieve and wash it in running water until the water runs clear. Tip it into an ovenproof dish that will hold the chicken in a single layer (I use a shallow cast-iron casserole, 12 inches in diameter). Add everything else, except the oil and pistachios, and toss around to mix, leaving the chicken pieces skin-side up and sprinkling them with salt.

Drizzle with the oil. Cook in the oven, uncovered, for 40 minutes. The top should be golden and the chicken cooked through. Scatter with the pistachios and serve with a green salad.

korean chicken, gochujang mayo & sweet-sour cucumber

GOD, THIS IS GOOD. I made it for a party in my back yard one year as it's great "hold in the hand" food and it's never been off the menu since. The chicken must be warm—not hot—or the mayo turns oily. Gochujang is Korean chile paste; it has a special flavor, sweet and hot with a hint of miso.

SERVES 6

For the chicken and marinade
3 fat garlic cloves, crushed
1 cup soy sauce
¼ cup light brown sugar
2 teaspoons rice vinegar
3 tablespoons sesame oil
8 to 12 skinless boneless chicken thighs

For the mayonnaise
½ cup mayonnaise
2 teaspoons gochujang
½ garlic clove, finely grated to a purée
good squeeze of lime juice, to taste

For the sweet-sour cucumber
1 cucumber
1 shallot, very finely sliced
¼ cup rice vinegar, or to taste
3 teaspoons superfine sugar, or to taste
1 red chile, seeded and finely sliced

To serve
6 buns or wraps, warmed
sprigs of cilantro

Mix all the ingredients for the chicken. Roll the chicken in this marinade, cover, and chill for four hours or so, turning the thighs over every so often. For the mayonnaise, just mix the mayo, gochujang, and garlic. Add lime juice to taste. Peel the cucumber, halve it lengthwise, and scoop out and discard the seeds. Slice finely, then mix it with the rest of its ingredients, adding 1½ tablespoons of water. Let stand for 30 minutes. Taste for sweet–sour balance, adding more vinegar or sugar if you like.

Lift the chicken out of the marinade, shaking off any excess. Heat a couple of skillets. Cook on high heat for a couple of minutes, turning frequently, then reduce the heat and cook until done right through (check by cutting into one of the thicker pieces) and lovely and dark gold. Put the chicken on a plate—add the juices as well, so the chicken stays moist—and let cool a little.

Fill the warm buns or wraps with chicken, cilantro, and cucumber. Slather with mayo. Serve.

chicken with haricots & creamy basil dressing

BEST LUKEWARM rather than hot, so it's good for summer. You can poach the chicken rather than sautéing (though remove the skin before serving if you poach it). Make the dressing just before you start the dish, as it discolors if it is left sitting for long. Don't get whacking great chicken breasts; medium-sized are better here.

SERVES 4

For the dressing
1¾oz basil leaves
½ small garlic clove, crushed
¾ tablespoon white balsamic vinegar
salt and pepper
⅓ cup extra virgin olive oil (fruity, not bitter)
⅓ cup heavy cream
1½ tablespoons lemon juice, or to taste

For the chicken
3 tablespoons olive oil
4 chicken breasts, skin on or off, as you like
5½oz green beans, topped but not tailed
2 shallots, finely sliced
14oz can of haricot beans, drained and rinsed
1 cup cherry tomatoes, halved
½ tablespoon lemon juice
2 tablespoons extra virgin olive oil

Make the dressing: put the basil into a food processor with the garlic, vinegar, seasoning, and extra virgin olive oil. Whizz until blended. Scrape into a bowl and stir in the cream and lemon juice. The mixture will thicken, so you may want to add a little water to let it down again. (Not too much, though. I like this spoonable rather than pourable.) Check the seasoning.

Now on to the chicken. Heat the regular olive oil in a large skillet, season the chicken, and fry it, (skin-side down if it's skin on), for four or five minutes, over medium–high heat to get a good color, then reduce the heat. Turn and cook for another four or five minutes. Cut into the chicken on the underside to check for doneness; the juices should be clear with no trace of pink. Set aside.

Boil or steam the green beans until tender but still al dente. Put these, the shallots, haricot beans, and tomatoes in a bowl and season well. Stir in the lemon juice and extra virgin olive oil. Divide between four plates and put a chicken breast on each. Spoon over the basil dressing.

parmesan roast chicken with cauliflower & thyme

THIS CAME ABOUT because I had a craving for roast chicken with cauliflower and cheese one night, but was too lazy to make it. The whole family fell for it and it has since become a staple. You could use a mixture of cheeses, for example, half Gruyère to replace some of the Parmesan, if you want something more melting and gooey on top.

SERVES 4

8 skin-on bone-in chicken thighs

¾lb baby round red or round white potatoes, halved

1 cauliflower, broken into good-sized florets

2 onions, cut into wedges

8 sprigs of thyme

¼ cup extra virgin olive oil

sea salt flakes and pepper

⅓ cup Parmesan cheese, finely grated

Preheat the oven to 400°F.

Put the chicken, potatoes, cauliflower, and onions into a roasting pan in which everything can lie in a single layer, or the chicken and vegetables will sweat instead of roasting. Tear in the thyme, pour in the oil, and season. Toss everything around with your hands, finishing with the chicken skin-side up. Sprinkle the chicken with sea salt flakes to help the skin crisp up.

Roast, tossing occasionally—you have to ensure that the cauliflower turns golden all over, not just on one side—for 35 minutes. Sprinkle with the Parmesan cheese, toss to combine, and roast for another 10 minutes. The chicken and potatoes should be cooked through, the onions slightly scorched at the tips, and the surface of everything golden.

burmese chicken with tart-sweet chile sauce

THIS IS FROM one of my favorite books, *Burma: Rivers of Flavor*, by Naomi Duguid. I've fiddled a little with the sauce, but that's it. This is one of the most addictive and easy dishes in the book. If you're not familiar with Naomi's work, seek it out. I have every book she's written.

SERVES 6

For the chicken
3lb skinless boneless chicken thighs
1 teaspoon ground turmeric
½ teaspoon salt
½ teaspoon cayenne pepper
¾-inch piece ginger root, peeled
    and grated
4 garlic cloves, grated
2 tablespoons fish sauce
2 tablespoons peanut oil

For the dipping sauce
¾oz dried red chiles (remove the
    seeds from half of them)
3 garlic cloves, minced
1 tablespoon fish sauce
3 tablespoons superfine sugar
2 tablespoons rice vinegar
really good squeeze of lime juice, plus
    lime wedges to serve

Put the chicken thighs in a dish and mix in all the other ingredients except the oil. Turn the meat over until completely coated. Cover and put in the fridge to marinate for 30 minutes, then return to room temperature.

Meanwhile, to make the dipping sauce, put the chiles in a saucepan with 1 cup of water. Bring to a boil, then reduce the heat and simmer for three to five minutes. Mix this (including the water) with all the other ingredients and either pulse–blend in a small food processor or pound in a mortar and pestle (you need to break down the chiles and garlic).

Heat the oil in a skillet and cook the chicken in batches. You need to start off over high heat to get a good color, then reduce the heat to medium–low to cook it through. Keep turning the chicken as it cooks. Serve with lime wedges and the dipping sauce and boiled rice.

chicken chettinad

INDIAN FOOD has a hard time when it comes to quick cooking, as
nearly every dish has quite a few ingredients. I now keep a container on
my kitchen counter with all my most frequently used spices in it; that
makes life a lot easier. This dish actually tastes better the day after you
cook it. It contains yogurt, so don't boil it. Instead, bring it to just under
a boil when you are reheating it, otherwise the sauce will split.

SERVES 4

For the chicken
1¼lb skinless boneless chicken thighs,
    cut into big chunks
1 cup plain yogurt
1½ teaspoons ground turmeric
½ teaspoon salt
2 tablespoons vegetable oil
2 onions, minced
1 teaspoon fennel seeds
1 cinnamon stick

8 garlic cloves, grated
2-inch piece ginger root, peeled and grated
1 teaspoon soft dark brown sugar
1 tablespoon coarsely chopped cilantro leaves

For the spice blend
¾ tablespoon fennel seeds
¾ tablespoon coriander seeds
½ tablespoons black peppercorns
1 teaspoon chili flakes

Put the chicken in a bowl with the yogurt, turmeric, and salt and stir together. Cover and let
marinate for 30 minutes. Meanwhile, put all the spices for the spice blend in a dry skillet over
medium heat and stir until they smell aromatic. Grind them in a small blender, or by bashing
in a mortar and pestle.

Heat the oil in a small cast-iron casserole or sauté pan and cook the onions until they are soft
and golden. Add the fennel seeds and cinnamon stick and cook for a couple of minutes, then
add the chicken, garlic, ginger, and spice blend. Turn everything over with a wooden spoon and
cook for four minutes, then add the sugar and ½ cup of water and bring to a gentle simmer.

Cook very gently for 15 minutes—the juices will thicken a little as the dish cooks—then scatter
with the cilantro and serve with rice and chutney.

chicken with indian spices, mango & coconut

I FIND THE COMBINATION of spices, mango, and coconut absolutely irresistible. And, yes, I am suggesting you use curry paste, otherwise it means an endless list of spices. Why make life hard? This dish works perfectly well with a paste.

SERVES 4

2 teaspoons unsalted butter

½ tablespoon peanut oil

6 skinless boneless chicken thighs, cut in half

salt and pepper

2 medium onions, coarsely chopped

3 garlic cloves, crushed

6 medium tomatoes, chopped

1½ tablespoons curry paste (I use Patak's vindaloo)

1 teaspoon ground ginger

1 cup chicken stock

⅔ cup canned coconut cream

1 teaspoon soft light brown sugar

1 just-ripe mango, peeled, pitted, and sliced

3 tablespoons heavy cream

juice of ½ lemon or 2 limes

2 tablespoons coarsely chopped cilantro leaves

Heat the butter and oil in a sauté pan, add the chicken, and cook until golden on both sides, seasoning it as it cooks. (You only want to color it, not cook it through.) Transfer to a plate.

Add the onions and garlic to the pan and cook over medium heat until soft, about 10 minutes. Tip in the tomatoes and cook for another three minutes. Stir in the curry paste and ginger. Cook for two minutes, until the spices have released their aromas, then add the stock, bring to a boil, and keep boiling until the liquid has been reduced by about half.

Reduce the heat, add the coconut cream and sugar, and return the chicken to the pan. Cook over medium–low heat (do not boil it) for 15 minutes. Add the mango in the last four minutes of cooking time.

Stir in the cream and add the citrus juice. Taste for seasoning. Simmer for about a minute to heat through, then add the cilantro and serve with rice.

VEGETABLES

roast squash with ricotta, smoked cheese & sage

A CROWN PRINCE squash is the one to go for here. It has a lovely color and a good sweet flavor. Do try to buy fresh ricotta, rather than the sterilized preserved stuff; you'll find fresh ricotta in delis or Italian grocery stores. Oak-smoked Cheddar is gorgeous with this.

SERVES 6

For the salad
3lb 5oz squash or pumpkin
1/3 cup olive oil, divided
freshly grated nutmeg
10½oz fresh ricotta
5½oz salad leaves, such as baby spinach, ruby chard,
    or watercress, coarse stalks removed
3½oz smoked cheese, shaved
18 to 24 sage leaves

For the dressing
¾ tablespoon white balsamic vinegar
smidgen of Dijon mustard
¼ cup extra virgin olive oil
salt and pepper

Preheat the oven to 375°F. Halve the squash, seed it, and slice the flesh into wedges about ¾ inch thick at their widest. Peel each wedge. Put the slices into a roasting pan with ¼ cup of the olive oil, the nutmeg, and salt and pepper, and toss to coat in the seasoning and oil. Roast for about 25 minutes, or until tender and slightly caramelized in places.

Make the dressing by whisking everything together, then season well. Break the ricotta into little chunks with a fork. Toss the leaves with two-thirds of the dressing and divide between six plates or put on one big platter. Add the roast squash, ricotta, and shaved smoked cheese.

Heat the rest of the olive oil in a skillet and quickly sauté the sage leaves until they are crisp. Scatter these over the top, then drizzle with the rest of the dressing and serve.

broccoli with harissa
& cilantro gremolata

WHEN PURPLE SPROUTING broccoli isn't in season, you can use broccolini instead. This is also lovely made with roast cauliflower (see page 244 for how to roast cauliflower).

SERVES 6 as a side dish

For the broccoli
1 stick unsalted butter, at room temperature
3½ teaspoons harissa
pinch of salt
squeeze of lime juice
30 spears purple sprouting broccoli

For the gremolata
1 small garlic clove, coarsely chopped
3 tablespoon chopped cilantro leaves
zest of 2 limes, removed with a zester

Mash the butter with the harissa, salt, and lime juice. Cook the broccoli—either boiling or steaming it—until just tender (test with the tip of a small sharp knife). The time it takes depends on the thickness of the spears.

Finely chop the ingredients for the gremolata together so that they're combined. Remove the broccoli spears from the pan and immediately put them into a clean dish cloth, to soak up some of the excess moisture. Put onto a warm platter with walnut-size lumps of the butter.

Allow the butter to melt a little, then scatter the dish with the gremolata.

ginger-miso pumpkin & mushrooms, black sesame

A LOVELY MIXTURE of sweetness, earthiness, and lip-smacking umami. I sometimes make a little extra of the miso mixture and use it to dress purple sprouting broccoli (which I add to this dish at the end). Brown rice is lovely on the side. This is so satisfying, you won't even think about meat.

SERVES 6

3lb pumpkin, such as Crown Prince, seeded, cut into wedges and peeled

¾-inch ginger root, peeled and grated

2 garlic cloves, grated

¼ teaspoon chili flakes

⅓ cup peanut oil

salt and pepper

3 tablespoons white miso

1½ tablespoons honey

2 tablespoons rice vinegar

3 teaspoons soy sauce

14oz large flat mushrooms (about 6)

2oz baby spinach

generous squeeze of lime juice

¼ tablespoon black sesame seeds

Preheat the oven to 400°F. Arrange the pumpkin in a single layer (more or less) in a roasting pan. Mix the ginger, garlic, chili flakes, 4½ tablespoons of the oil, and seasoning and add it to the pumpkin, turning to make sure it is well coated. Roast for 30 minutes. Mix the miso, honey, rice vinegar, and soy sauce together with 1½ tablespoons of warm water.

Arrange the mushrooms in a separate roasting pan and add the remaining oil, turning the mushrooms over in it. Put one-third of the miso mixture on the mushrooms and put them into the oven. Add the rest of the miso to the pumpkin, turning all the vegetables over in it. Roast for another 30 minutes along with the mushrooms.

At the end of cooking time, add the spinach to the pumpkin and turn it over in the cooking juices; it should wilt a little in the heat. Transfer all the vegetables to a warm, broad, shallow serving bowl. Squeeze some lime juice over the whole dish and scatter with the sesame seeds.

roast sweet & bitter vegetables, salsa bianca

I LOVE THE TASTES of bitter and sweet together, and it's even better when there's something salty added to the mix. This sauce is Italian, but I do sometimes make it with Scandinavian sweet-cured anchovies. The result is different, but also very good.

SERVES 8 as a side dish, 4 as a main course

For the vegetables
8 carrots, halved lengthwise (quartered if very fat)
1½lb cauliflower, broken into florets
2 beets (not too big), trimmed and cut into wedges
about 8 sprigs of thyme
3 onions, cut into thick wedges
⅓ cup olive oil, plus extra for brushing
salt and pepper
1 head of radicchio, cut into 6 wedges
2 heads of red or white Belgian endive, quartered

For the salsa bianca
½ cup pine nuts
1¾oz can of anchovies in olive oil, drained
1 fat garlic clove, crushed
½ cup extra virgin olive oil
lemon juice, to taste

Preheat the oven to 375°F. Put the carrots, cauliflower, beets, thyme, and onion wedges into a roasting pan in which they can lie in a single layer (you want them to roast, not sweat). Drizzle with the regular olive oil, season, and turn the vegetables over to make sure they all get well coated. Roast for about 25 minutes, turning them over every so often, then brush the radicchio and endives with a little more regular olive oil and add to the pan. Roast for another 15 minutes, or until all the vegetables are tender and slightly burnished in patches.

To make the salsa, dry-fry the pine nuts in a skillet until golden and smelling toasted. Tip into a mortar and pound with the anchovies and garlic, then start adding the extra virgin olive oil, a little at a time. Season and add the lemon juice to taste. You should have a coarse paste. It's strong, but good with this. Serve the vegetables with the salsa on the side.

roast cauliflower with spanish flavors

I ATE A DISH very like this at Opera Tavern in Covent Garden, in London, and couldn't get it out of my head. I tried to recreate it quite a few times, but something always seemed missing. So, I contacted the chef, Ben Tish, and he gave me his recipe. The following is a blend of both our approaches. If you like it, the credit goes to Ben.

SERVES 4 as a side dish or "small plate"

½ cup raisins

1 cup amontillado sherry

1 large head of cauliflower, broken into good-sized florets

2 onions, cut into 1-inch wedges

8 sprigs of thyme

½ teaspoon ground cinnamon

1 teaspoon cumin seeds

⅓ cup extra virgin olive oil, divided, plus extra to taste (optional)

salt and pepper

2 garlic cloves, finely sliced

¼ teaspoon chili flakes

½ tablespoon sherry vinegar

good squeeze of lemon juice, or to taste

3 tablespoons toasted pine nuts (see page 242)

Put the raisins in a saucepan with the sherry and bring to a boil. As soon as it reaches boiling, take the pan off the heat and let the raisins plump up for about 30 minutes.

Preheat the oven to 400°F. Put the cauliflower and onions into a roasting pan in which everything can lie in a single layer. Tear in the thyme coarsely and add the cinnamon, cumin, 3 tablespoons of the olive oil, and seasoning. Toss all this around with your hands and put it in the oven for 35 minutes. Toss occasionally during cooking to ensure the cauliflower becomes golden all over, not just on one side.

Halfway through cooking, add the garlic, chili flakes, and raisins with their soaking liquid and mix. When the cauliflower is tender and golden, remove it from the oven. Set the roasting pan over medium heat and add the sherry vinegar, the rest of the olive oil, and the lemon juice. Gently toss around and warm through. Taste: you might find you need a little more lemon juice or oil, or to adjust the seasoning. Transfer to a warm platter, scatter with the pine nuts, and serve.

peperoni gratinati al forno

JUST WHEN YOU THOUGHT you were aware of everything that could be done with roast bell peppers, along comes this from southern Italy. I've described it as a side dish (it is great with lamb) but, in fact, a lunch of these bell peppers, served tepid, with burrata is more feast than side dish.

SERVES 6 as a side dish

8 red bell peppers, halved and seeded, stems removed

extra virgin olive oil

8 cured anchovies, drained and chopped

2 tablespoons chopped black olives

2 tablespoons capers, rinsed

leaves from 2 sprigs of oregano, torn

2 small garlic cloves, grated

¼ teaspoon chili flakes (optional)

⅓ cup stale bread crumbs

Preheat the oven to 350°F. Put the bell peppers into a roasting pan, brush with olive oil, and cook in the hot oven for 30 minutes. Remove from the oven.

Increase the oven temperature to 375°F.

Cut the bell peppers into strips and toss with the rest of the ingredients in a bowl, reserving some bread crumbs for the top. Put the mixture into a gratin dish or other shallow ovenproof dish. Sprinkle with the rest of the crumbs, drizzle with more olive oil, and put back into the oven for another 15 minutes, or until the crumbs are golden. Serve.

sweet potatoes with yogurt & cilantro-chile sauce

HOT, SWEET, COOL, all the contrasts I love are in this dish. You can use the yogurt and sauce for baked sweet potatoes; just split them and fill with a spoonful of each.

SERVES 6 as a side dish

For the sweet potatoes
2¼lb sweet potatoes, scrubbed really well
   and cut into thick wedges
¼ cup olive oil
½ tablespoon honey
juice of 1 lime
salt and pepper
1 cup Greek yogurt
extra virgin olive oil

For the sauce
2 garlic cloves, chopped
2 green chiles, seeded and chopped
2 tablespoons blanched almonds
leaves from 1 medium bunch of cilantro,
   about ½oz
⅓ cup extra virgin olive oil
juice of 1 lime
1 tablespoon white balsamic vinegar

Preheat the oven to 350°F.

Put the sweet potatoes into a roasting pan. Mix together the regular olive oil, honey, lime juice, and seasoning and toss this with the potato wedges. Cook for 30 to 35 minutes, until tender.

Put everything for the sauce into a food processor and pulse-blend, to form a coarse purée. Put the potatoes into a warm serving dish. Spoon the herb sauce and some of the yogurt over the wedges, drizzle with extra virgin olive oil, and serve with the rest of the yogurt.

creamy gratin of rainbow chard & red Belgian endive

I LOVE A CREAMY vegetable gratin—who doesn't?—but they can be a little cloying. In this dish, the endive's slight bitterness cuts through the richness. You can omit the anchovies if you hate them, but they don't taste fishy once it's all cooked, and they just end up giving the dish a bit of an umami hit.

SERVES 4 as a side dish

1lb 2oz rainbow chard or regular chard

1 tablespoon unsalted butter

salt and pepper

1 small onion, minced

olive oil

1 small head of red Belgian endive, leaves
  separated and chopped

4 anchovies, drained and chopped

1 garlic clove, crushed

1 cup heavy cream

¾ cup finely grated Parmesan cheese, divided

¼ cup bread crumbs

Preheat the oven to 400°F.

Pull the leafy parts off the chard, trim the stalks, and cut them into pieces 1½ inches long. Put the stalks in a big pan of boiling water and cook for three minutes, adding the leaves after two minutes. Drain. Dry the leafy bits in a dish cloth (but don't squeeze them as you might spinach).

Melt the butter in a skillet, add a little salt, and sauté the onion for about six minutes, until soft but not colored. Add a splash of olive oil and the endives, anchovies, and garlic and cook until the endives have softened, about three minutes. Now put the chard leaves and stems into the pan and stir them around to get well flavored in the fat. If the chard is still a little watery, increase the heat to high to drive off the moisture. Reduce the heat to medium again and pour in the cream, then add ½ cup of the Parmesan cheese and plenty of pepper (you probably won't need salt because of the anchovies, but taste to check).

Transfer the mixture to a gratin dish, sprinkle with the remaining Parmesan cheese and the bread crumbs, and bake for 20 to 30 minutes. The top should be golden.

olive oil-braised leeks
& peas with feta & dill

USE CRUMBLED RICOTTA and mint here instead of feta and dill,
if you prefer. Just be sure to cook the leeks gently. I've suggested
having this as a side dish, but actually it makes a lovely main
course with another vegetable dish and couscous or bulgur wheat.

SERVES 4 as a side dish, or as a main course with a spread of other vegetable dishes
4 large leeks
⅓ cup extra virgin olive oil, plus more to serve
⅓ cup light chicken or vegetable stock
1 garlic clove, crushed
salt and pepper
1 cup peas, fresh or frozen
finely grated zest of ½ unwaxed lemon
1 tablespoon coarsely chopped dill fronds
⅔ cup crumbled feta cheese

Remove the coarser outer leaves from the leeks and trim the tops. Cut into pieces 1½ inches
long, discarding the bases. Wash really well, so you get rid of any trapped soil.

Heat the oil in a heavy saucepan or sauté pan and gently cook the leeks over medium heat
for about seven minutes. Don't let them color. Add the stock and garlic, bring to a boil, then
immediately reduce the heat to low, season, and cover with a lid. Cook for 10 to 12 minutes,
until the leeks are just tender (check with the point of a knife).

Add the peas and cook until they are tender (frozen peas need very little cooking, as they more
or less just heat through). Scatter with the lemon zest and check for seasoning. Transfer to a
bowl (a shallow one looks best) and scatter with the dill and feta. Drizzle with more oil to serve.

tomatoes, potatoes & vermouth with basil crème fraîche

BAKING ROUND RED OR ROUND WHITE POTATOES can be problematic. They seem to become tender at different rates depending on the variety, so you may have to cook this a little longer than suggested. You want to end up with the right amount of liquid, too, because the vegetables should be just coated in thickish juices, not swimming in them. It's a simple dish, but requires a bit of judgment.

SERVES 6 as a side dish

2 red onions, halved

1lb 5oz baby round red or round white potatoes, halved lengthwise

1¾lb plum tomatoes, halved

⅓ cup extra virgin olive oil

3 tablespoons white balsamic vinegar

finely grated zest of 1 unwaxed lemon, plus juice of ½

4 garlic cloves, crushed

salt and pepper

½ cup dry vermouth

1¼ cups crème fraîche

leaves from a small bunch of basil, torn

Preheat the oven to 440°F. Cut the onions into crescent-shaped wedges (about ¾ inch at their thickest part) and put them into a really big roasting pan that can hold all the vegetables in a single layer. Add the potatoes, tomatoes, oil, vinegar, lemon zest, garlic, and seasoning and toss everything around with your hands. Finish with the tomatoes cut-side up.

Roast for 45 to 60 minutes, pouring in the vermouth 20 minutes before the end of cooking time. (Round potatoes vary in the length of time they take to cook, and they need to be tender.) There will probably be liquid—vermouth and cooking juices—around the vegetables. Put the roasting pan over high heat on the stove and simmer until some of this has boiled off. It doesn't matter if the tomatoes get softer and lose their shape as you do this.

Check the seasoning and transfer to a heated serving dish. Mix the crème fraîche with the lemon juice and basil. Serve the vegetables with the cream on the side.

asparagus, goat cheese & warm butter

DON'T USE STRONG goat cheese for this, as it will overwhelm the delicate asparagus. A milder cheese, creamy or chalky in texture, is what you want.

SERVES 4 as a main course, 6 as an appetizer
2¼lb asparagus spears
¾ stick unsalted butter
juice of 1 lemon
12oz rindless goat cheese, broken into chunks
salt and pepper

Break or cut the woody ends from the asparagus spears. Bring about 3 inches of water to a boil in a saucepan and put the bases of the asparagus spears in this, leaning the upper parts against the inside of the pan (or use an asparagus cooker if you have one, or steam them). Cook until just tender but still a little firm. This should take about four minutes, but it depends on the thickness of the spears.

Meanwhile, melt the butter and add the lemon juice to it. Lift the asparagus out and drain before dividing among individual plates (or serve on a platter). Scatter with the cheese, sprinkle with salt and pepper, and drizzle with some of the lemon butter. Put the rest of the butter in a pitcher and serve with good bread.

artichokes, carrots & preserved lemons with ginger & honey

AN INTERESTING DISH. Instead of throwing all the ingredients—without liquid—into the oven, I tried something more like a vegetable braise, but didn't cook it on the stove. It has Moroccan flavors (preserved lemons and honey) but French touches, too (bay and vermouth). I can eat this on its own as a main course, but it's also a lovely side dish for lamb. You can add peas or fava beans, but that rather ruins the muted colors.

SERVES 6 as a main course

10½oz young carrots, ideally slim
1lb 2oz baby round red or round white
  potatoes, halved
12 shallots, peeled and halved
1 head of garlic, cloves separated and peeled
½ tablespoon peeled and finely grated ginger root
¾ teaspoon Aleppo pepper or cayenne pepper
1 teaspoon coriander seeds, coarsely crushed
about 6 sprigs of thyme, plus leaves from 2 more

3 preserved lemons, flesh discarded,
  rind shredded
4 bay leaves
½ cup extra virgin olive oil
½ cup vermouth
1¾ cups vegetable stock
14oz can of artichoke hearts, drained
2 tablespoons honey

Preheat the oven to 350°F. Peel the carrots and trim the tops. If they're slim leave them whole, otherwise halve them lengthwise. Put everything except the artichokes, extra thyme leaves, and honey into a big roasting pan. The vegetables should lie in a single layer. Set over medium heat and bring the liquid just to a boil. Immediately put it into the oven and cook for 45 minutes. Gently turn the vegetables over once or twice during this time.

Drain and dry the artichoke hearts using paper towels, then halve them. Add to the vegetables and cook for a further 15 minutes. Drizzle with the honey, scatter with the remaining thyme, and cook for a final 15 minutes. You should have soft vegetables with olive oil-rich, well reduced juices.

salty baked potatoes
with yogurt

I KNOW THIS MIGHT SEEM RIDICULOUS: a recipe for baked potatoes. But there is a right way to do them so that you end up with a crisp skin and a fluffy interior. They might be simple, but they're worth doing well.

SERVES 6

6 medium floury Idaho potatoes, weighing about 10½oz each (Russet Burbank, Russet Arcadia, Russet Norkotah, and Butte are all good varieties for baking)
sea salt flakes and pepper
unsalted butter
Greek yogurt

Preheat the oven to 400°F.

Scrub the potatoes and prick with a fork. While they are still damp, sprinkle lightly all over with the sea salt flakes. This gives a crisp skin (cooking them wrapped in foil gives them a soft skin).

Put the potatoes on a baking pan—they shouldn't touch one another—then wet your hands and splash the pan with water. Bake in the oven for 1 to 1½ hours (the exact cooking time depends on size and how many potatoes you are cooking at once; a bigger quantity of potatoes sometimes takes longer). To test whether the potato is done, press it: it should feel soft under the skin and give a little. You can put a fine skewer right through to the center of the potato if you want to be sure.

Make a cross in the top with a sharp knife and firmly press the potato (hold it in a dish cloth while you do this) so it opens at all four points. Season with salt and pepper and put a walnut-size lump of butter in the middle, then a dollop of yogurt.

one potato, two potato...

The first baked potatoes I ever tasted—odd for an Irish girl—were in Canada. I thought the mix of hot potato flesh, melting butter, cool sour cream, and chopped scallions was irresistible. At university (where a weekly essay crisis required all-night working) I'd trudge to the baked potato vendor on a street nearby at about 2 A.M. When there was frost or snow underfoot you couldn't wait to get your hands around the warm Styrofoam box. Shoveling in potato, baked beans, and grated cheese was so comforting. It's often hard, when you're hungry, to think of interesting fillings for baked potatoes, though. So here are a few of my favorites. I still have baked beans and Cheddar cheese—it tastes of the past, apart from anything else—but I can often do a bit better than that.

CASHEL BLUE, WALNUTS & WATERCRESS
Split open your potato. Fill with a handful of watercress (it will wilt and that's fine), a dollop of sour cream, crumbled Cashel blue cheese or Roquefort, and a sprinkle of toasted walnuts.

SOUR CREAM, SMOKED TROUT & DILL
A classic and as good as ever, but best in smaller potatoes (it seems very rich in a big one). Put a walnut-size lump of butter in your split potato, then sour cream, flaked smoked trout, and chopped dill. To be indulgent, a spoon of keta (salmon roe) is gorgeous on top.

BACON LARDONS, ONIONS & GRUYERE
Fry bacon lardons—chunky ones—in the fat that runs out of them as they cook. Set aside and sauté finely sliced onions in the fat until soft and golden (or take them to dark gold by increasing the heat). Fill your split potato with the onions, bacon, and, finally, grated Gruyère cheese. To get the Gruyère to melt into those gorgeous long strings, put the potato under a hot broiler. This is pretty good with a fried or poached egg on top as well (what a feast).

DAL, YOGURT & SPICY BUTTER
My student standby dish, but I make it better now. Make some dal (see page 77); you don't have to use pumpkin, just increase the amount of lentils. Fill a potato with this, plain yogurt (not Greek), and chopped cilantro. Melt butter in a skillet and add cumin seeds and chili flakes, plus chopped ginger root and garlic, if you can be bothered. Pour over the yogurt.

YOGURT, AVOCADO SALSA & FETA
Fill a baked sweet potato with a big spoonful of Greek yogurt and another of chopped avocado mixed with chopped tomatoes, lime juice, some finely chopped chile, ground cumin, and olive oil. Top with chopped cilantro leaves and coarsely crumbled feta cheese.

GOAT CHEESE & BLACK OLIVE RELISH
Chop pitted black olives and mix with chopped walnuts, parsley, garlic, and chile. Add olive oil and white balsamic vinegar. Squeeze on some lemon juice. Put crumbled goat cheese and arugula into a split baked sweet potato and spoon the relish on top. Grind on pepper.

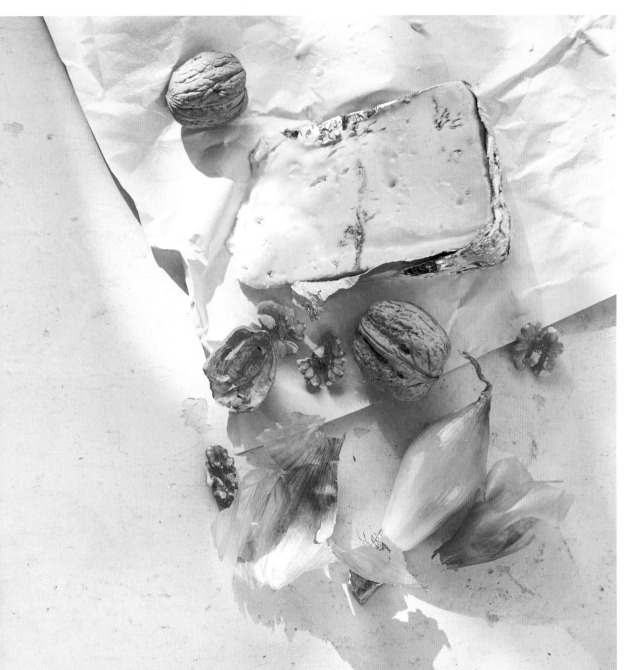

HAM, CAMEMBERT & CREAM

Bake your potato, then take the flesh out of
it and mash it. Cook some minced onion in
butter, then add cooked ham (the chunks you
get at the deli counter are good), seasoning, and
cream. Mix with chopped camembert (or grated
Cheddar or Gruyère) cheese and return to the
potato skins. Broil or bake until golden.

SMOKED HADDOCK, CHEDDAR & SPINACH

Poach smoked haddock in milk until almost
cooked. Wilt spinach in butter and cook until
the water mostly evaporates. Chop. Mash the
spinach with the flesh from the baked potatoes,
the haddock, butter, some cream, seasoning,
and grated Cheddar cheese. Pile back into the
skins and brown under the broiler.

baked sweet potato, chorizo, mushrooms & egg

SWEET *and* earthy—always a winning combination. You can omit the egg, or use bacon lardons instead of chorizo, if you prefer. A great, gooey, savory-sweet plateful.

SERVES 2

2 sweet potatoes
3 tablespoons extra virgin olive oil
5½oz cremino mushrooms, cleaned, chopped into pieces
salt and pepper
3½oz chorizo, sliced a little thicker than ⅛ inch
2 large eggs
small handful of cilantro leaves (optional)
sprinkling of smoked paprika (optional)

Preheat the oven to 400°F.

You bake sweet potatoes in the same way as regular potatoes, but for only about 30 minutes (though I find cooking time varies according to the texture of the variety you're using). Be careful to bake them in a foil-lined pan, as they leach a sticky liquid that is hell to shift.

When the potatoes are nearly cooked, heat 1 tablespoon of the olive oil in a skillet and sauté the mushrooms briskly over fairly high heat. Season. Mushrooms give out a lot of moisture when they cook, so make sure these juices have evaporated. Scrape into a bowl and keep warm. Add ½ tablespoon more oil to the pan and brown the chorizo on both sides. Add to the mushrooms.

Heat the rest of the oil and fry the eggs, scooping hot oil up over the yolks to help them cook.

Split each potato lengthwise to open them up. Spoon the mushrooms and chorizo inside the potatoes and scatter with the cilantro. Top with the fried eggs—sprinkling on a little smoked paprika, if you want—and serve with baby leaves, such as spinach.

butternut strata

A STRATA IS an Italian savory bread pudding, a generous, melting dishful that is great for lunch or supper with friends. If you want a vegetarian version, just omit the bacon and use more squash. You can add cooked leeks or spinach, but make sure they're well drained.

SERVES 8

2¼lb butternut squash

3½ tablespoons olive oil, divided, plus more for the sage

salt and pepper

9oz ricotta, preferably fresh

1½oz sourdough bread without crusts

2 cups whole milk

6 large eggs, lightly beaten

generous grating of nutmeg

about 15 sage leaves, divided

⅔ cup finely grated Parmesan or pecorino, divided

1 onion, minced

2 garlic cloves, minced

7oz bacon lardons

unsalted butter, for the dish

4½oz buffalo mozzarella, drained, torn

Preheat the oven to 400°F. Seed the squash and cut into 1-inch wedges. Peel and put into a roasting pan. Toss with 2 tablespoons of the olive oil and season. Roast until tender and slightly caramelized (about 35 minutes). Let cool. Drain the ricotta in a sieve.

Tear the bread into a bowl, add the milk, eggs, and ricotta and loosely mash. Add the nutmeg, half the sage (chopped), and ¼ cup of the Parmesan cheese. Season well. Cover and chill.

Sauté the onion in 1 tablespoon of the olive oil until soft and pale gold, then add the garlic and cook for another minute. Set aside. Using the remaining ½ tablespoon of oil, sauté the bacon until golden all over.

Butter a baking dish and put half the bread and milk mixture into it. Add half the squash, all the mozzarella, and half the bacon and onions. Ladle on the other half of the bread mixture, then the remaining bacon and onions, then the rest of the squash. Sprinkle with the remaining Parmesan cheese. Let stand for 30 minutes (this gives a lighter dish).

Preheat the oven to 350°F. Put the dish in a roasting pan and add enough boiling water to come one-third of the way up the sides of the dish. Cook for one hour. Fry the remaining whole sage leaves in very hot olive oil for a few seconds (they will turn crispy) and scatter these on top. Serve with a green salad.

roast beets with goat cheese, rye & dill

You'll find it hard to believe, when you look at how many beets you have, that it will only feed four or six people, but they do shrink. There are loads of ways you can go with roast beets: mix dill with yogurt and spoon it over instead of goat cheese, followed by freshly grated horseradish; try a dill-scented gremolata; or go to another area of the world entirely and top with thick yogurt, cilantro, or dill and slivers of preserved lemon. Serve these while still a little warm.

Serves 4 as an appetizer, 6 as a side dish

1lb 10oz mixed beets (regular, golden, and candy cane if you can get them), preferably the size of golf balls
olive oil
½ cup buttermilk
3 tablespoons canola oil
salt and pepper

2 tablespoons chopped dill fronds
1¾oz rye bread or pumpernickel, whizzed into crumbs
8oz soft goat cheese, crumbled
handful of seeds (flax or pumpkin), if you have them

Preheat the oven to 400°F. Trim the leaves from the beets and wash the beets thoroughly. Leave the little straggly tips at the base if you can, but they need to be well cleaned. Put into a roasting pan and drizzle generously with olive oil. Toss everything around with your hands, then add about 3 tablespoons of water. Roast until completely tender. This can take 30 minutes or it can take up to an hour, depending on the size of the beets.

Mix the buttermilk with 2 tablespoons of the canola oil, the seasoning, and dill. When the beets are cool enough to handle, peel off the skins, cut in half lengthwise, and put in a serving dish.

Heat the remaining canola oil in a skillet and fry the bread crumbs until crisp and smelling like toast. Drizzle the beets with the buttermilk mixture, then scatter the goat cheese and bread crumbs on top. Sprinkle with the seeds, if using, to serve.

biberli cacık

You can't get much simpler than this, but the combination of sweet flesh and tart dressing is irresistible. Use regular bell peppers if you can't find Turkish or Romano (though they're a lovely shape).

Serves 4

8 long Turkish peppers, or Romano peppers if you can't get those
¼ cup olive oil
salt and pepper
4 small red chiles, seeded
1 cup Greek yogurt
¼ cup buttermilk
2 tablespoons extra virgin olive oil, plus more to serve
1 garlic clove, crushed
3 tablespoons coarsely chopped dill fronds
½ cup crumbled feta cheese

Preheat the oven to 400°F. Put the peppers into a roasting pan and drizzle with the regular olive oil. Season. Roast in the oven for 25 to 30 minutes, until they are completely tender, adding the chiles halfway through (tuck them in under the peppers).

Meanwhile, mix the yogurt with the buttermilk, extra virgin olive oil, and garlic. The mixture should be thin enough to drizzle.

Put the peppers on a serving plate, pouring any cooking juices from the roasting pan over them. Chop the chiles and scatter them on top. Spoon on the yogurt mixture, then scatter with the dill and crumbled feta cheese. Drizzle with a little more extra virgin olive oil and serve.

roast potatoes with chili, mint & preserved lemon

STARCHY SIDES are the last thing I think about when preparing a meal and I often just stick little round potatoes tossed in olive oil into a hot oven. It's good to have a range of ideas for flavoring them. These are so good I could eat them on their own, but they're also great with any meat (or other vegetable dishes) inspired by the Middle East. You could add some pitted, chopped green olives just before the end of cooking.

SERVES 6 as a side dish
1½ preserved lemons
2¼lb baby round red or round white potatoes
¼ cup olive oil
salt and pepper
½ teaspoon chili flakes
3 garlic cloves, minced
about 20 mint leaves, torn

Preheat the oven to 400°F.

Remove the flesh from the preserved lemons (discard it) and cut the rind into slivers. Set aside.

The potatoes should be about the size of a walnut (unshelled). If they're larger, then halve them. Put these into a gratin dish, or a small roasting pan, where they can lie in a single layer. Pour on 3 tablespoons of the olive oil, season, and toss the potatoes around in the oil to coat.

Roast them in the oven for 30 minutes, tossing in the chili flakes after 15 minutes. The potatoes should be tender right through. Using the remaining tablespoon of olive oil, gently fry the garlic until pale gold. Toss into the potatoes, mixing well, followed by the mint and the preserved lemon rind.

baby potatoes with watercress & garlic cream

POTATOES GET OVERLOOKED, but you can make them special with very
little effort. This is most definitely not a salad; the watercress will wilt
a little in the heat of the potatoes. It's a good mixture of temperatures
and an excellent side dish for so many things, such as plain roast lamb
or chops, chicken, or fish.

SERVES 8 as a side dish
2¼lb baby potatoes
1 tablespoon unsalted butter
squeeze of lemon juice
salt and pepper
1 cup half-fat crème fraîche (half-fat just has a good texture for this)
1 small garlic clove, crushed
2½ cups watercress, coarse stalks removed
¾ cup very thinly sliced radishes, ideally a mixture of pink and purple

Boil the potatoes until tender, then slice coarsely and place in a serving dish. Add the butter and
lemon juice and toss to coat. Season well.

Mix the crème fraîche with the garlic, and then season it. Add the watercress to the potatoes
(it will wilt a little, but that's good) and scatter with the radish slices. Spoon over some of the
crème fraîche mixture and offer the rest in a bowl at the table.

roast eggplants
with crushed walnuts
& anchovies

GOOD WITH ROAST LAMB, or with a range of vegetable dishes served as
a main course. You can roast eggplants like this—scoring the flesh makes
all the difference—and serve them with things that take less effort. Try a
chickpea purée (see page 89), or have a look at my selection of quick sauces
and relishes (see pages 152–153). Eggplants are so meaty—really satisfying—
and go with such a range of flavors.

SERVES 6 as a side dish, 4 as a main course with other vegetables
8 eggplants
olive oil
sea salt flakes and pepper
1 fat garlic clove, chopped
1¼ cups walnut pieces
5 anchovies, drained of oil and chopped
⅓ cup extra virgin olive oil
2 tablespoons lemon juice, or to taste
1 teaspoon white balsamic vinegar
3 tablespoons finely chopped parsley leaves

Preheat the oven to 375°F. Halve the eggplants lengthwise. Make a crisscross pattern on the cut
sides, without cutting through, to help heat penetrate. Put into a roasting pan where they can lie
in a single layer. Brush them with regular olive oil and season. Roast for 25 minutes.

Grind the garlic and a pinch of salt to a paste in a mortar (salt flakes act as an abrasive). Add the
walnuts and anchovies and pound until you have a mixture that is part-puréed and part-chunky.
Stir in the extra virgin olive oil, lemon juice, vinegar, pepper, and the parsley.

Take the eggplants out of the oven, turn them over, then return to the oven for 10 minutes.
Transfer to a platter, cut-sides up, and spoon on the walnut and anchovy mixture.

fragrant sichuan eggplants

THIS IS BASED ON a glorious Sichuan dish in which the eggplants
are deep-fried. However, I don't trust myself to deep-fry when I'm in
a hurry, so I've changed it. If you don't have Chinese black vinegar,
use balsamic. The chile bean paste can be found in some large
supermarkets, Asian grocery stores, or online (I've also used Korean
chile paste when stuck. It's not Sichuan but it's still damned good). This
is thickened with potato flour, but I sometimes leave it out as the sauce
can be quite thick enough.

SERVES 4 as a side dish

4 eggplants

¼ cup peanut oil

generous 1½ tablespoons Sichuan chile bean
  paste (*douban jiang*)

¾-inch piece ginger root, peeled and grated

1 red chile, seeded and shredded

4 garlic cloves, minced

½ cup chicken stock or water

1½ teaspoons superfine sugar

2 teaspoons soy sauce

salt and pepper

¾ teaspoon potato flour

2 teaspoons Chinese black vinegar

4 scallions, trimmed and cut into
  pieces 2 inches long

white sesame seeds

Take the tops off the eggplants. Cut each into three sections, then cut each section into thick
batons. Heat 1½ tablespoons of the oil in a wok and, over high heat, cook half the eggplants
until they're well colored and soft. Remove and set aside. Repeat to cook the rest of the
eggplants. Set aside.

Heat the remaining tablespoon of oil in the wok and add the chile paste. Cook for 20 seconds,
then add the ginger, chile, and garlic. Cook for 30 seconds, then add the stock or water, sugar,
soy sauce, and seasoning. When the mixture comes to a simmer, return the eggplants to the wok
and cook for a couple of minutes until they absorb the sauce. Mix the potato flour with
1 tablespoon cold water until smooth.

Add the vinegar, scallions, and potato-flour mixture to the wok and cook for 30 seconds or so.
Taste for seasoning. Sprinkle with sesame seeds and serve immediately with rice.

roast eggplants with tomatoes & saffron cream

IT MIGHT SEEM ODD to mix eggplants—a very Mediterranean vegetable—with cream, but it works here, making a truly luscious dish that is soft, rich, and luxurious. Depending on what else you are offering, you can serve this as it is, or scatter shaved Parmesan on top. It's very good indeed with roast lamb but you can increase the quantities and serve it as a main course, too. Let the saffron soak for a good 30 minutes before you use it, to develop a much better color and flavor.

SERVES 6 as a side dish

very generous pinch of saffron stamens

3 eggplants

extra virgin olive oil

6 sprigs of tomatoes on the vine
 (4 to 5 tomatoes on each)

salt and pepper

1 tablespoon unsalted butter

2 shallots or ¼ onion

⅔ cup dry white wine or dry vermouth

2 cup strong chicken or vegetable stock

⅔ cup heavy cream

lemon juice, to taste

Put the saffron in a cup and stir in 3 tablespoons of boiling water. Set aside for 30 minutes.

Preheat the oven to 375°F. Halve the eggplants lengthwise. Cut a cross-hatch pattern on the cut sides, without cutting through (this helps heat penetrate so they roast more quickly). Put into a roasting pan where they and the tomatoes can lie in a single layer. Brush the eggplants with olive oil and drizzle some more on the tomatoes. Season. Roast for 30 minutes.

Melt the butter in a saucepan and cook the shallots until soft but not colored. Add the wine and boil to reduce to about 3 tablespoons. Add the saffron water and stock and boil until reduced by two-thirds. Add the cream and bring to a boil. Season and boil until the sauce can coat the back of a spoon. Strain to remove the shallots. Add a little lemon juice and check the seasoning.

Take the vegetables out of the oven, turn the eggplants over, then roast for a final 10 minutes. Transfer to a warm platter or broad shallow bowl (eggplants cut-side up) and spoon over some of the cream. Serve the rest of the cream on the side.

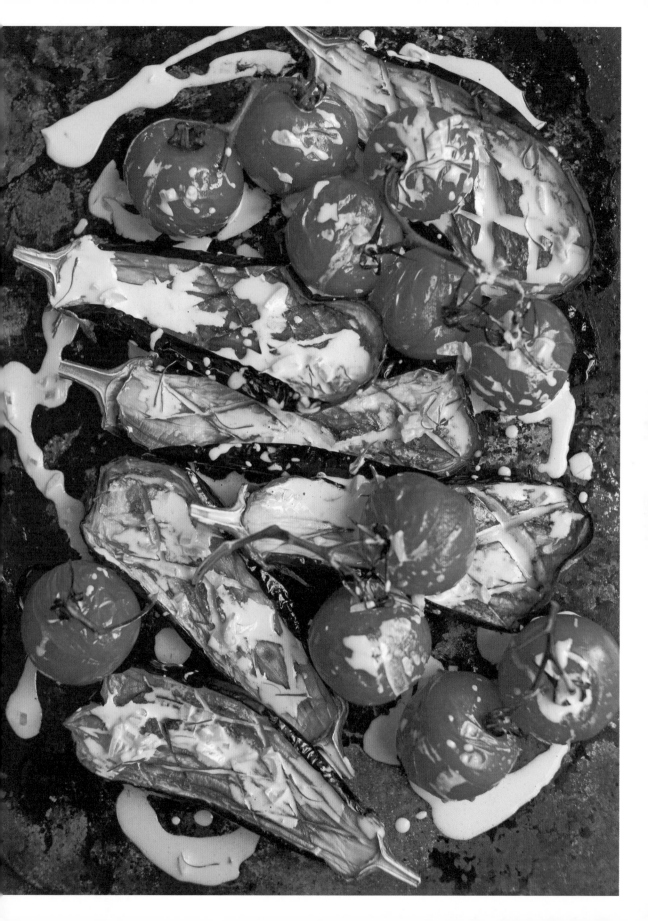

FRUIT
DESSERTS

pears baked with lemon, bay & marsala

ELEGANT—EVEN IF IT'S RUSTIC—subtle, autumnal. The bay leaves make all the difference.

SERVES 6

6 fat, just-ripe pears
2½ cups Marsala
juice of 1 unwaxed lemon, plus the zest of ½, removed in broad strips
6 bay leaves
1 cup soft light brown sugar

Preheat the oven to 375°F.

Halve the pears lengthwise. Lay them, cut-side up, in a single layer in a shallow ovenproof dish. The dish should just hold the pears, without lots of room around, otherwise the Marsala will simply evaporate. I don't core or peel the pears. If they have stalks leave those on, too.

Pour on the Marsala and lemon juice with ½ cup of water, tuck the lemon zest under the fruit, and add the bay leaves. Sprinkle ¾ cup of the sugar on top of the pears and around them. Bake for 40 to 45 minutes, or until the pears are tender and starting to wrinkle at the edges. From time to time during cooking, spoon the juices over the top of the pears. Add the remaining ¼ cup of sugar toward the end of cooking time. You should have a glossy brown sweet sauce around the pears but, if it looks as if it is toffee-ish and thick, add a little more water. Put the pears in a serving dish, or serve them in the dish in which they've been cooked.

Serve with crème fraîche. You could offer hazelnut or almond cookies on the side.

roast apple &
maple eton mess

A BIT OF OLD ENGLAND with a big dollop of New England. Have the various components ready, but don't assemble this until you're about to serve or the meringues go mushy.

SERVES 6

1½lb cooking apples, peeled, cored, and halved

¼ cup soft light brown sugar

⅓ cup maple syrup, divided, plus more to serve

3½ tablespoons hazelnuts

1 cup heavy whipping cream

⅓ cup Greek yogurt

4¼oz meringue, coarsely broken up

Preheat the oven to 400°F. Put the apples into a roasting pan and sprinkle with the sugar. Pour about 3 tablespoons of water over the apples. Roast for 15 to 20 minutes, or until the fruit is completely tender. Drizzle 3 tablespoons maple syrup over the apples and let cool. Tip the hazelnuts into a dry skillet, place over medium heat, and toast until they smell aromatic. Remove from the heat and coarsely chop.

Break the apples up coarsely using a fork; you still want texture. Whip the cream until it holds its shape, then stir in the yogurt and the remaining maple syrup.

Layer the apples, cream, hazelnuts, and meringue in glasses, drizzling them with maple syrup as you go. Finish with a layer of cream, a drizzle of maple syrup, and some hazelnuts.

roast apricot & orange blossom fool

THE FLAVOR of roast apricots is incredibly intense and honeyed, so it can easily cope with being "softened" by cream. Serve with amaretti or *langues de chat* cookies.

SERVES 8

1¾lb apricots, halved and pitted

⅓ cup white wine or water

1 teaspoon vanilla extract

½ cup granulated sugar

1¼ cups heavy cream

¼ cup Greek yogurt

⅓ cup orange blossom honey, or to taste, plus more to serve

1 tablespoon orange flower water, or to taste

toasted sliced almond, to serve

Preheat the oven to 375°F. Put the apricots in a gratin dish, cut-side up, in which they can lie in a single layer. Mix the wine or water with the vanilla in a small bowl and pour it over the fruit, then sprinkle evenly with the sugar.

Roast in the oven for 30 to 45 minutes (it depends how ripe the fruit is), or until completely soft. Let stand until cold. Remove some of the best-looking apricot halves to put on top of each serving. Purée the rest of the fruit and all its juice (there won't be much) in a food processor.

Whip the cream—don't let it get too stiff—then stir in the yogurt, honey, and flower water. Combine with the apricot purée, but don't mix it so much that you lose the bright orange of the apricots; leave the fool slightly marbled. Taste for sweetness and to check if you want to add more flower water.

Spoon into glasses or bowls. Add an apricot half to each, if you want, drizzle with a little more honey—depending how sweet you found it—then scatter with toasted sliced almonds to serve.

summer berries
in mint julep syrup

BERRIES, BOURBON, MINT. What's not to like? Make sure the
syrup is good and cold.

SERVES 6 TO 8

1 cup bourbon, divided

1 cup granulated sugar, or to taste

juice of 4 limes, divided, or to taste

about 40 mint leaves, divided, plus more sprigs of mint to serve

2lb mixed berries: strawberries, blueberries, raspberries, and red currants

Put ¾ cup of the bourbon into a pan with the sugar and half the lime juice. Add ⅔ cup water
and bring to a boil, stirring a little to help the sugar dissolve. Add half the mint leaves and boil
until reduced by half. Remove from the heat and pour in the remaining lime juice and bourbon.
Taste—you may want more sugar or a little more lime—then let cool. Strain to remove the
mint, then chill.

Hull the strawberries and cut into slices about ⅛ inch in thickness. Put into a bowl with the
rest of the berries and currants and pour over the chilled syrup and the remaining mint leaves.
Put in the fridge for about 30 minutes. If you leave it there any longer the fruit gets too soft.
Serve with whipped cream, adding a sprig of mint to each serving.

peaches in peach
tea with rosemary

HERBAL AND INTENSELY PEACHY. You could use lavender instead of rosemary, if you prefer.

SERVES 6

2 peach tea bags (or another fruit tea; berry or apple would work)

⅔ cup granulated sugar

3 sprigs of rosemary, plus more to serve

juice of 2 lemons, plus 2 broad strips of unwaxed lemon zest

6 freestone peaches, halved and stone removed

Put the tea bags into a pitcher with 4 cups of boiling water and let brew for about seven minutes. Discard the tea bags and pour the tea into a saucepan large enough to take all the peaches in a single layer. Add the sugar and stir to dissolve. Add the rosemary, lemon juice and zest, and peaches. Bring to a simmer and gently poach the peaches until they are tender. This will take 12 to 25 minutes, depending on how ripe your peaches are. Keep checking, sticking the tip of a sharp knife into the hollow where the peach stone was.

Scoop out the peaches with a slotted spoon and set them on a dish so that they are not touching (if you pile them on top of one another they will continue to cook and soften).

Remove the lemon zest and one of the sprigs of rosemary from the poaching liquid, then bring the liquid to a boil and cook until it is reduced to a syrup; you should have about 1 cup of liquid. Set aside to cool completely, leaving the rosemary in the syrup.

Put the peaches into a serving dish and strain the syrup over them. Add a few fresh sprigs of rosemary to serve.

summer fruit & almond cake

A LOVELY CAKE for August or September, when fruit is abundant. You can use a different fruit mixture—peaches, blackberries, and figs would be good, too—as long as the stone fruit is ripe.

SERVES 8

For the cake

1 stick unsalted butter, softened, plus extra
   for greasing
⅔ cup superfine sugar
2 large eggs, lightly beaten
1 teaspoon vanilla extract
½ teaspoon almond extract
1½ cups all-purpose flour
¾ teaspoon baking powder
½ cup sour cream
½ cup marzipan, broken into little chunks
pinch of salt

For the fruit

2 ripe nectarines, halved, stone removed,
   and sliced
1 large or 2 smaller unripe plums, halved,
   pitted, and sliced
½ cup raspberries
3 tablespoons superfine sugar
a little confectioners' sugar, to dust

Preheat the oven to 375°F. Butter an 8-inch springform cake pan and line it with nonstick parchment paper.

Put all the ingredients for the cake into a food processor and whizz until smooth. Scrape the batter into the prepared pan.

Toss the fruit with the superfine sugar and then lay the pieces, higgledy-piddledy, on top of the batter.

Bake for 1½ hours. The cake is ready when a skewer inserted into the middle comes out clean (although the marzipan does make it hard to judge this cake, which is rich and moist). Let cool in the pan, then carefully unlatch the sides and remove the base. Peel off the paper and transfer the cake to a plate. Dust lightly with confectioners' sugar to serve.

berries & melon in elderflower syrup

THE ELDERFLOWER SYRUP here is very useful: you can poach apricots or little halved apples in it, or pour it onto sliced ripe peaches or mangoes.

SERVES 6

1¾ cups white wine

1 cup granulated sugar

juice of 1 lemon, plus 2 broad strips of unwaxed lemon zest

2 tablespoons elderflower cordial, or to taste (they vary considerably in strength)

½ Chanterais or Ogen melon

1½ cups strawberries, hulled and halved or quartered (leave very small berries whole)

1½ cups raspberries

Mix the wine, sugar, and lemon juice and zest together with 1 cup of water in a saucepan and slowly bring to a boil, stirring a little to help the sugar dissolve. Boil for seven minutes. Remove from the heat and add the cordial, then let cool completely. You should have a light syrup. Strain.

Remove the seeds from the melon and cut the fruit into slices. Remove the skin from each slice and place into a broad, shallow bowl with the strawberries and raspberries. Pour over the cooled syrup. Chill briefly (if you let the fruit stand in the syrup for too long the fruit gets unpleasantly soft), or serve at room temperature with whipped cream or crème fraîche.

baked plums in sloe gin

SIMPLICITY ITSELF. If you have some damson gin lying around,
that works well, too. And pears are good instead of plums.

SERVES 4

12 plums, halved and pitted

½ cup sloe gin, plus 1½ tablespoons to serve

juice of 1 orange, plus 2 broad strips of orange zest

5 juniper berries, crushed

⅓ cup soft light brown sugar

Preheat the oven to 400°F.

Put the plums into a roasting pan in which they can lie snugly in a single layer, cut-side up. Mix the gin and orange juice and pour it over the fruit. Tuck the orange zest and juniper berries in under the fruit. Sprinkle with the sugar and bake for 20 minutes, or until tender.

Using a slotted spoon, lift the plums out of the roasting pan and into a serving dish to cool. Don't pile them on top of one another, otherwise they continue to cook and can get too soft.

Put the roasting pan over high heat and bring the juices to a boil. Cook until they've reduced and look slightly syrupy. Be careful, though: if you've used a pan where there's quite a lot of room around the fruit, the juices will have evaporated more and may already be thick enough. They will thicken more as they cool. Chill, then pour the juices over the plums with the extra 1½ tablespoons sloe gin, just to boost the booziness.

sherry-roasted pear
& chocolate sundaes

PEARS, SHERRY, CHOCOLATE, this is a heady and wonderful mixture.
You don't have to serve it in sundae glasses, of course, just use what
you have. The important thing is to be generous. And be careful not to
overheat the chocolate sauce; go slowly and keep everything warm, not
hot, and all will be well.

SERVES 8
8 under-ripe pears, halved and cored
2 cups sweet sherry
juice of 1 lemon
⅓ cup soft dark brown sugar
7oz high-quality semisweet chocolate (70% cocoa solids), broken into pieces
½ cup whole milk
3 tablespoons heavy cream
¼ cup superfine sugar, plus 1½ tablespoons
2 tablespoons unsalted butter
1 cup heavy whipping cream
1 teaspoon vanilla extract
vanilla ice cream, to serve
⅓ cup hazelnuts, halved and toasted (see page 281)

Preheat the oven to 375°F. Arrange the pears, cut-side up, in a single layer in a shallow ovenproof
dish. Pour the sherry, lemon juice, and ⅓ cup of water over the pears. Sprinkle with the brown
sugar and bake for 40 to 45 minutes, or until tender. Let cool.

Put the chocolate in a heatproof bowl and melt over a pan of simmering water. Separately
heat the milk, heavy cream, and ¼ cup of superfine sugar, stirring to help the sugar melt.
Slowly whisk the milk into the melted chocolate; at first it will look as though it won't blend
in, but keep beating and it comes together. Whisk in the butter until it melts. Let cool a little;
it is good if the sauce is warm. Beat the whipping cream and vanilla with the 1½ tablespoons
superfine sugar.

Assemble the sundaes, in sundae glasses or dessert dishes, arranging the pears with some
vanilla ice cream, nuts, and chocolate sauce. Top with whipped cream, a final drizzle of
chocolate sauce, and more hazelnuts.

hot cherries with grappa & ice cream

I ATE THIS in a restaurant in Norcia in Umbria. I traveled most of the day to get there because Claudia Roden, writing in *The Observer* newspaper, had recommended it. It was the most modest place and the food—a tomato and basil salad, lamb chops *scottadito* with fried potatoes, sausages with lentils, and this pudding—has stayed with me. It was a perfect meal. The owners had no idea that Claudia had recommended them and were so thrilled that they thanked us with more grappa than we could drink. (And ran around Norcia on a Sunday night trying to find a photocopier to copy Claudia's piece. I left it with them.) This is a last-minute dessert and some people hate serving those—they like to have everything organized before their friends arrive—but it takes very little time and there's something lovely about taking warm cherries to the table in a skillet.

SERVES 4

2 tablespoons unsalted butter

3 cups pitted sweet cherries (I like to tear them rather than cut them to remove the pits)

½ cup superfine sugar

juice of ½ lemon

3 to 4 tablespoons grappa

vanilla ice cream, to serve

Melt the butter in a large skillet, then add the cherries and any juices that came out of them when you were pitting them. Toss them around over medium heat, adding the sugar and stirring gently to help it dissolve. Add the lemon juice. Keep tossing the cherries and cooking until they have a thickish syrup around them.

Add the grappa (you can now flambé the cherries if you want, but it's not necessary) and you're done. Take to the table and serve cold ice cream with the hot cherries.

white nectarines & raspberries in rosé

A REALLY ELEGANT PUDDING. Peaches can be used instead, but I like the slight tartness of nectarines, and the fragrance of the white-fleshed fruits.

SERVES 6

2½ cups rosé wine

1 cup granulated sugar, plus 2 tablespoons

2 strips of unwaxed lemon zest, plus the juice of ½ lemon

6 white nectarines or freestone peaches, halved and stone removed

1½ cups raspberries

Put the wine, sugar, lemon zest, and juice in a pan big enough to hold the nectarines, preferably in a single layer. Bring to a boil, stirring to help the sugar dissolve, then reduce the heat. Add the nectarines and poach gently, turning them over every so often, until they are just tender. Start checking after eight minutes, then keep checking because they can get soft quite suddenly. Remove the fruit as it's ready and let cool lying in a single layer. Then boil the poaching liquid until it is reduced and slightly syrupy. You want to end up with 1 to 1¼ cups. Set aside until cold; the liquid will thicken more as it cools.

Carefully remove the skins from the nectarines (they should just slip off). Pour the cold syrup over the nectarines and chill.

Just before serving, gently stir in the raspberries, being careful not to break them up.

rhubarb & raspberry crumble cake

VERY MOIST, this makes as good a dessert as it does a cake to serve with coffee or tea.

SERVES 8

For the cake
1¼ sticks unsalted butter, more for the pan
½ cup superfine sugar, plus ⅓ cup more
   for the fruit
3 large eggs, lightly beaten
2 teaspoon vanilla extract
1 cup all-purpose flour sifted with
   1 teaspoon baking powder
2 tablespoons milk (optional)
1½lb rhubarb, trimmed and cut into 1-inch pieces
1 cup raspberries
confectioners' sugar, to dust

For the crumble
1½ cups all-purpose flour
1 stick cold unsalted butter, cubed
½ cup superfine sugar
1 cup sliced almonds

Preheat the oven to 350°F. Butter a 9-inch springform cake pan.

Beat the butter and the ½ cup sugar together until pale and fluffy. Add the eggs a little at a time, beating well after each addition, then add the vanilla. If the mixture starts to curdle, stir in 1 tablespoon of the flour. Fold in the remaining flour, then add enough milk to give the batter a reluctant dropping consistency. Scrape into the prepared pan.

Toss the rhubarb and raspberries with the ⅓ cup superfine sugar and spread it evenly over the top of the cake batter. For the crumble, rub the flour and butter together with your fingers until the mixture resembles bread crumbs. Stir in the sugar and almonds, then scatter the mixture over the fruit.

Bake for one hour 20 minutes. When it is done, the top should be golden and a skewer inserted into the middle of the cake should come out clean. Let cool in the pan, then carefully unlatch the sides and remove the base. Dust with confectioner's sugar to serve.

apricot & amaretti crostata

LIKE FREE-FORM TARTS, crostatas are very forgiving. If the pastry tears as you are shaping it or crimping the edges, just patch it up. You can use ground almonds, walnuts, or hazelnuts instead of the amaretti cookies (and omit the liqueur, too). You could also make this tart with peaches or plums instead.

SERVES 8 TO 10

2¼ cups all-purpose flour, plus more to dust

1½ sticks unsalted butter, chilled and cut coarsely into cubes

¾ cup sifted confectioners' sugar, plus more to serve

1 egg yolk

1 tablespoon heavy cream

1 cup amaretti cookie crumbs

2 tablespoons granulated sugar, divided

1lb 5oz apricots, pitted and quartered (neither over-ripe nor very under-ripe)

2 tablespoons lemon juice

2 tablespoons amaretto liqueur (optional)

Put the flour, butter, and confectioners' sugar into a food processor and whizz until you have a mixture like bread crumbs. Add the egg yolk and cream and whizz again. It should come together into a ball. If it doesn't, add a couple of teaspoons of very cold water and whizz again. Seal in plastic wrap and put in the fridge to rest for an hour; longer is fine, too.

When ready to bake, preheat the oven to 375°F. Roll out the pastry into a circle, about 13 inches across, on a lightly floured piece of nonstick parchment paper. Mix the amaretti crumbs with half the granulated sugar. Leaving a 1½-inch border all the way around, sprinkle on the amaretti mixture. Lay the apricots on top in a higgledy-piggledy fashion. Sprinkle on the remaining sugar followed by the lemon juice and the liqueur, if using. Pull the edges of the pastry up around and over the edges of the fruit and pinch it slightly all the way around, or just pinch it up to make a higher rim. Patch it up if it breaks. Slide, still on its parchment paper, onto a cookie sheet. Bake for 35 minutes. If the pastry gets too dark, cover it with foil. The fruit should be tender and slightly singed in parts. Let cool a little, then dust with confectioners' sugar to serve.

melon granita

THERE AREN'T MANY DESSERTS EASIER to make than a granita.
You just need a fork and a freezer. Melon granita should be strongly
perfumed, so use perfectly ripe melons. Charentais is the best variety
for this, and has a gorgeous color, too. The last time I made this
was in the middle of a heatwave. I forgot about it until one night
when I was testing recipes very late and had the oven on. I suddenly
remembered this was stashed away in the freezer and ate a bowl of it,
in the garden, after midnight, the granita melting almost faster than
I could eat it. It was bliss.

SERVES 6
1¼ cups superfine sugar
2 Charentais melons
juice of 3 limes, or to taste

Bring 1 cup of water to a boil, then take it off the heat and add the sugar. Stir until the sugar
has dissolved, then set aside to cool.

It's important to capture every bit of juice from the melons, so cut them on a board set on a
tray with a lip all the way around. Halve the melons and remove the seeds. Scoop the flesh
out with a spoon into a bowl. Set a sieve over the bowl and put all the juice that's collected
in the tray into the sieve, along with the seeds and the fibers around them. Press lightly to
extract more juice.

Whizz the melon flesh and all the juice you've collected in a food processor. Push it through
a sieve. Combine this purée with the sugar syrup and the juice of 1 to 2 limes. Taste. You'll
probably need the juice of the other lime, but you don't want to spoil the delicate taste of the
melon by going too far, so use your judgment.

Put into a shallow container and place in the freezer. Drag a fork through the mixture every
so often as it is freezing, to create icy shards. Serve just as it is, in little chilled glasses.

roast apple, blackberry & whiskey trifles

THERE'S NO CUSTARD, I know, but these qualify as little trifles in my book. You could add a layer of custard if you wanted to, though; a good ready-made carton of fresh custard would be fine. Double the quantities if you want to make a single trifle in a big bowl.

SERVES 4

1lb 3oz cooking apples, peeled, cored, and quartered

¼ cup soft light brown sugar, plus 1½ tablespoons for the cream

about 36 blackberries

1½ tablespoons superfine sugar

½ cup apple juice

¼ cup granulated sugar

¼ cup whiskey, divided, or to taste

1 cup heavy cream

16 ladyfingers

3 tablespoons halved hazelnuts, toasted (see page 281)

Preheat the oven to 400°F. Put the apples into a roasting pan and sprinkle with the ¼ cup of soft light brown sugar. Roast in the oven until the apples are completely tender, about 30 minutes. They will burst and look quite messy, but that's okay. Put them, and their juices, into a bowl and mash with a fork. Let cool.

Set aside some blackberries for decoration and toss the rest in a bowl with the superfine sugar. Put the juice in a small pan with the granulated sugar and bring to a boil, stirring to dissolve the sugar. Let cool, then add 2 tablespoons of the whiskey. Whip the cream and stir in the remaining 1½ tablespoons soft light brown sugar and 2 tablespoons of whiskey. Get four glass dessert dishes, cups, or bowls ready.

Halve the ladyfingers and dip half of them into the apple syrup. Keep them there until they are really soggy but haven't fallen apart, then lay them in the glasses. Add a layer of apple purée, then some cream, then soak the other half of the ladyfingers in syrup and place them on top.

Divide the blackberries that have been sitting in sugar among the four glasses. Spoon some of the apple syrup onto each serving, shaking it to help it run down into the layers. Top with more cream and scatter with hazelnuts and the reserved blackberries.

baked apples with marmalade & southern comfort cream

IF YOU THINK Southern Comfort tastes like cough medicine (or too much like adolescence) then use whiskey, bourbon, apple brandy, or a little Cointreau instead. Everyone likes a baked apple, but they do need something to make them a little special.

SERVES 8

For the apples
1 cup golden raisins and black raisins
1¼ cups orange juice, divided
finely grated zest of 1 orange
8 eating apples, preferably with stalks
¾ cup coarsely chopped hazelnuts or walnuts,
   lightly toasted (see page 281)
1 cup soft light brown sugar

For the marmalade cream
1¼ cups heavy cream
⅓ cup marmalade, not too firmly set
confectioners' sugar, to taste
1½ tablespoons Southern Comfort, or to taste

Put the dried fruit in a saucepan with half the orange juice and bring to a boil. Reduce the heat and simmer for about five minutes, then take the pan off the heat, add the zest, and let the fruit stand for about 30 minutes to plump up. Preheat the oven to 350°F.

Slice the top off of each apple to make a lid about 2 inches across, then core the rest of each fruit. Remove a little of the flesh around the core, too, so there is room for the stuffing. Put them in an ovenproof dish. Mix the plumped-up dried fruit with the nuts and brown sugar. Spoon the stuffing into each apple, sprinkling leftovers around the dish, and put the apple lids back on. Pour on the remaining orange juice. Bake for 30 to 40 minutes, or until completely tender, spooning any juices over every so often (keep an eye on them, as they get to bursting stage very suddenly).

Whip the cream until it just holds its shape, then beat in the marmalade until it has broken down. Add the confectioiners' sugar (you won't need much) and Southern Comfort, or whatever booze you are using. Serve the apples warm, with their cooking juices and the whipped cream.

marmalade baked fruit with boozy orange cream

So EASY. Use a marmalade with fine shreds if you can. It's important that both the pears and the plums are slightly under-ripe, otherwise they will overcook and fall apart before the apples are tender.

SERVES 6

For the fruit
2 slightly under-ripe, long, skinny pears
juice of 2 lemons
2 apples
6 slightly under-ripe plums, halved and pitted
finely grated zest of 1 orange
⅓ cup orange marmalade
1½ tablespoons maple syrup
2 tablespoons sherry or whiskey

For the cream
1 cup heavy whipping cream
finely grated zest of ½ orange
1 tablespoon soft dark brown sugar
Cointreau, to taste

Preheat the oven to 375°F.

Quarter the pears lengthwise and core the pieces. You don't need to peel them. Put them in a large ovenproof dish from which you can serve (or a roasting pan is fine; you can transfer them to a serving dish later). Immediately pour the lemon juice onto the pears. The pieces of fruit (including the apples and plums) shouldn't be piled on top of one another, but should lie in a single layer. Halve and core the apples and cut each half into four wedges. Add to the pears followed by the plums and the orange zest. Mix the fruit around with your hands to ensure it gets covered in juice.

Stir together the marmalade, syrup, and alcohol, using the back of a spoon to break the marmalade down. Spoon this all over the fruit and bake for 40 minutes, or until the fruit is tender and slightly caramelized, basting with the cooking juices every so often.

To make the cream, whip it until it is beginning to thicken, then add the zest and sugar. Whip again until it is holding its shape well, then gradually add the Cointreau. Serve the fruit warm or at room temperature, with the cream on the side.

st. clements & rosemary posset with blackberries

POSSET IS A WONDER. All you do is heat cream, add citrus juice, and let cool and yet you end up with a silky, rich dessert. You can top this with any fruit—blueberries, poached rhubarb, raspberries—as long as it's quite tart.

SERVES 6
2 cups heavy cream
1 sprig of rosemary
¾ cup superfine sugar
juice of 1 lemon and ½ orange
blackberries, to serve

Put the cream, rosemary, and sugar into a heavy saucepan and slowly bring to a boil, stirring from time to time to help the sugar dissolve. Take it off the heat and let stand to infuse for 30 minutes. Remove the rosemary, place the cream mixture back onto the heat, and bring to a boil. Then reduce the heat slightly and let the cream bubble away for three minutes (you need to watch it like a hawk, in case it boils over).

Pour into a bowl and whisk in the citrus juices. Divide the mixture between six small glasses or cups and let cool, then cover and refrigerate. The posset will firm up, but needs to be in the fridge for about three hours.

Just before serving, put some blackberries on top of each posset.

no-hassle desserts

I love planning and cooking desserts, but rarely make anything very complicated. That's less to do with a shortage of time and more to do with the fact that simple desserts are among the best, especially when fruit is good. None of the following sweet endings are remotely taxing.

FRAISES MAM GOZ

A Breton strawberry dish. Heat ⅔ cup each red wine and water with ½ cup granulated sugar, stirring a little. Boil for seven minutes. Let cool then add a little orange flower water, to taste. Pour the mixture over hulled and halved strawberries. Let stand for 1 hour before serving.

MEL I MATO

A Catalonian way with dried fruit. Serve a mild, creamy goat cheese with dried fruit, toasted almonds or hazelnuts, a drizzle of thyme honey, and a glass of chilled Muscatel.

BERRIES, MERINGUES & CURD CREAM

Mix whipped cream with good-quality orange or lemon curd and the pulp of a few passion fruits. Serve big, ready-made meringues with the cream spooned over them, scattered with mixed berries.

ROAST BANANA & BROWN SUGAR FOOL

Put 5 really ripe, peeled bananas in an ovenproof dish with the finely grated zest and juice of 2 limes, plenty of soft dark brown sugar, and a good slug of dark rum. Bake in a medium oven for about 1 hour. Cool, then mash with 1 cup whipped heavy cream and some Greek yogurt. Add more rum or sugar to taste and chill before serving.

BAKED PEACHES WITH AMARETTO

Bake halved and stoned ripe peaches, topped with soft brown sugar and splashes of amaretto liqueur, in a hot oven for 30 minutes, or until tender to the point of a knife. Serve with whipped cream mixed with a good slug of amaretto liqueur, then sprinkle the whole thing with crumbled amaretti cookies.

WHITE NECTARINES WITH MUSCAT

If you can find perfectly ripe white nectarines, nothing is better than this. Halve the nectarines and remove the stone. Serve on a platter with white currants (they look like glowing pearls). Serve with glasses of very cold Muscat de Beaumes de Venise.

BLACKBERRIES & CRÈME DE CASSIS

Put blackberries in a bowl (you can mix them with black currants, too) sprinkle with superfine sugar, and gently stir in a couple of tablespoons of crème de cassis. Serve with a mound of ricotta or crème fraîche, or with scoops of vanilla ice cream.

BROILED APRICOTS & HONEY

Halve and pit ripe apricots, put them in a gratin dish, and drizzle with honey. Put these under a hot broiler and cook until bubbling (be careful not to let it go too far). Serve with crème fraîche and chopped pistachios.

PEACH MELBA

Make a raspberry sauce by whizzing 1½ cups raspberries with ¼ cup confectioners' sugar in a food processor. Push through a sieve, to remove the seeds. Layer perfectly ripe—or poached (see page 296)—peaches in tall glasses with the sauce and scoops of vanilla ice cream.

RASPBERRY-CHOCOLATE SUNDAE

Layer scoops of vanilla ice cream in a tall glass with crumbled, gooey-centered brownies, raspberries, and the raspberry sauce above. Finish with softly whipped cream. For a boozy version, add crème de framboise to the sauce.

RASPBERRY & WHISKEY TRIFLE

Put two slices of good spongecake—spread with raspberry jam—into shallow soup bowls and douse with whiskey mixed with a little sugar. Spoon some good, ready-made vanilla custard on top, followed by raspberries and sweetened whipped cream.

CHOCOLATE BARK

Melt high-quality dark or white chocolate. Pour on a tray lined with nonstick parchment paper. Top white chocolate bark with freeze-dried raspberries, blanched almonds, pistachios, and dried rose petals. Top dark chocolate bark with toasted hazelnuts, chopped dried apricots, and candied orange; or dried sour cherries and walnuts. Break into shards once hardened.

OTHER SWEET THINGS

sgroppino

I KNOW, I KNOW, barely a recipe and some would argue it's a cocktail rather than a dessert anyway. However you want to classify it, this is a pretty magnificent end to a meal. A sgroppino is a Venetian invention and it should, properly, be shaken and served in a foamy froth, but I like the look of the sorbet floating in the glass and, in any case, the sorbet quickly melts, producing a froth on its own. The pureness of lemon sorbet is very pleasing, but even in Venice they serve different flavors now. Peach or raspberry sorbet are good. And I've seen the odd fresh raspberry added, too.

SERVES 6
6 scoops of really good-quality lemon sorbet
6 glasses of chilled prosecco, only half filled
6 tablespoons vodka

Add the sorbet to the half glasses of prosecco carefully, as the wine will froth up. (When it has died down a little, you can top off with more wine.) Add a tablespoon of vodka to each glass, too, and serve.

lemon & lavender cake

You can now buy dried edible lavender. Check online if you cannot find it locally. If you want proper icing, use the glacé icing recipe from later in this chapter (see page 327).

Serves 8
unsalted butter, for the cake pan
1½ cups granulated sugar
¾ tablespoon edible dried lavender
1½ cups all-purpose flour
½ teaspoon baking powder
½ teaspoon baking soda
¼ teaspoon salt
2 large eggs, lightly beaten
1 cup Greek yogurt
½ cup mild-flavored olive oil
finely grated zest of 1 unwaxed lemon, plus 1 tablespoon lemon juice
confectioners' sugar, to dust
sprigs of fresh lavender, to serve

Preheat the oven to 350°F. Butter an 8-inch diameter, 2½-inch deep cake pan and line the bottom with baking parchment.

Put the granulated sugar and lavender into a food processor and whizz until the lavender has broken down. Sift the flour, baking powder, baking soda, and salt together into a bowl. Stir in the lavender sugar. In a pitcher, mix the eggs with the yogurt and oil. Make a well in the center of the dry ingredients and gradually stir in the wet ingredients. Add the lemon zest and juice, but don't over-mix. Scrape the batter into the prepared pan.

Bake for 45 to 50 minutes, or until the cake is coming away from the inside of the pan and a skewer inserted into the middle comes out clean. Turn it out, peel off the paper, and set on a wire rack until cold. Dust with confectioners' sugar just before serving and decorate with sprigs of fresh lavender.

bitter flourless chocolate cake with coffee cream

I'VE MADE SO MANY versions of this cake over the years that I could now bake it in my sleep. It's the little black dress of puddings: elegant and timeless. Do it a few times and it will become easy. Serve with a marmalade cream (see page 305) instead of the coffee version, or simply with summer berries and cream, or Hot cherries with grappa (see page 294).

SERVES 8

For the cake
1⅔ sticks unsalted butter, plus more for the pan
11½oz high-quality dark chocolate
   (70% cocoa solids), broken into pieces
¾ cup superfine sugar
5 large eggs, separated
½ cup ground almonds
confectioners' sugar, to dust

For the cream
1¼ cups heavy cream
½ tablespoon instant espresso coffee dissolved
   in ½ tablespoon boiling water
2 tablespoons whiskey, or to taste
3 tablespoons confectioners' sugar, or to taste

Preheat the oven to 350°F. Butter an 8-inch springform cake pan.

Put the chocolate, butter, and sugar into a heatproof bowl set over a pan of simmering water (the bowl shouldn't touch the water). Melt the mixture, stirring a little. Remove the bowl and let it cool for about four minutes. Stir in the egg yolks, one at a time.

Beat the egg whites with an electric hand-mixer until they form medium peaks (stiff but with the peaks drooping slightly). Using a big metal spoon, fold the ground almonds into the chocolate mixture along with half the egg whites, then fold in the rest of the whites.

Scrape the batter into the prepared pan and bake for 35 minutes. Cool completely, carefully unlatch the sides of the pan, and remove the base. Transfer the cake to a serving plate. It will deflate and crack as it cools. Whip the cream until just holding its shape, then drizzle in the coffee and whiskey, still whipping. Add the confectioners' sugar and taste for sweetness and booziness. Dust the cake with confectioners' sugar and serve with the cream.

roopa's kheer with scented fruits

I CAN'T REALLY write a book without including a few recipes from my friend Roopa Gulati. I love her food so much. She brought this rice dish to my house, but we talked so much that day we never got around to eating it. She wouldn't take it home, but left it in the fridge. I confess I ate it for breakfast for the rest of the week (indulgent, I know). Serve the rice thick, but not stodgy.

SERVES 8

For the kheer
generous pinch of saffron strands
10 cardamom pods
3 pints whole milk, more if needed
1 cup basmati rice
¾ cup pistachios, shelled, plus more to serve
1 cup superfine sugar, more if needed
½ to 1 tablespoon good-quality rose water
3 tablespoons thick heavy cream

For the dried fruit
1 cup superfine sugar
2 broad strips of orange zest
1 cup raisins, or a mixture of dried fruit
    including raisins, chopped apples, sour
    cherries, and chopped apricots
juice of ½ lemon or 1 lime
1 teaspoon rose water, or more to taste

Soak the saffron in 3 tablespoons of just-boiled water for at least 30 minutes. Split the cardamom pods, add to the milk in a heavy pan, and bring to scalding point. Stir in the rice, reduce the heat, and simmer for 30 to 40 minutes, until tender and thick. Stir often; add more milk if needed.

Finely chop the pistachios, or blitz them in a food processor. Add the sugar to the rice and stir until dissolved, then stir in the nuts and saffron with its soaking liquid. Let cool, then chill. It will get thicker so if it's already thick, you'll need more milk and possibly more sugar. Stir the rose water into the chilled rice—very gradually in case it is strong—with the cream.

For the dried fruit, heat 1 cup of water with the superfine sugar and orange zest, stirring to help the sugar dissolve. When it comes to a boil, take it off the heat and add the fruit. Let cool in the syrup. Once it's cold, add the citrus juice and rose water (go easy with the latter).

Spoon into small bowls. Scatter with pistachios to serve and offer the fruit on the side.

espresso loaf cake with burnt butter & coffee icing

THIS IS DENSER THAN REGULAR coffee cake, as it's made by the melt-and-mix method. I use a coffee extract for it. If you can't find any, you can use Camp Coffee, available in most supermarkets or online.

SERVES 10

For the cake
2¼ sticks unsalted butter, plus more for the pan
¾ cup strong coffee, preferably espresso
1½ cups soft light brown sugar
½ cup maple syrup
2 teaspoons coffee extract
2 large eggs, lightly beaten
2 cups all-purpose flour
1 cup malted brown flour, or wholemeal

pinch of salt
1 teaspoon baking soda
¾ cup coarsely chopped walnuts

For the icing
2 tablespoons instant espresso powder
1 stick unsalted butter
2 cups sifted confectioners' sugar
2 tablespoons toasted walnuts, chopped
  (see page 112)

Preheat the oven to 340°F. Butter a loaf pan measuring 9 x 5 x 2½in and line the bottom with nonstick parchment paper.

Put the coffee in a pan with the butter, sugar, and syrup. Heat gently, without boiling, stirring to dissolve the sugar. Pour into a pitcher and let cool. Whisk in the coffee extract and eggs.

Sift the flours, salt, and baking soda into a bowl, then add the bran from the sieve. Toss in the walnuts. Make a well in the dry ingredients and slowly pour in the wet mixture, stirring together gradually. Scrape into the prepared pan and bake for one hour 15 minutes. A skewer inserted into the center should come out clean. Let cool in the pan for 10 minutes, then turn out onto a wire rack and peel off the paper. Turn the cake the right way up and let it cool.

Dissolve the espresso powder in 2 tablespoons of boiling water and let cool. Melt the butter in a pan, then increase the heat and cook until it has just turned brown and nutty. Let cool. Put the butter in an electric stand mixer with the confectioners' sugar and beat, gradually adding the coffee. Cover and chill to firm up.

Using a metal spatula, spread the icing over the cake. It's a tea cake, so fancy embellishments aren't quite right, but you can scatter it with the toasted chopped walnuts.

lemon & ricotta cake

VERY MOIST because of the ricotta, though for the same reason it
doesn't keep fantastically well. Try to eat it within a day of being made.
It's the perfect cake with which to welcome spring.

SERVES 8
1¾ sticks unsalted butter, softened, plus more for the pan
1 cup superfine sugar
finely grated zest of 4 unwaxed lemons, plus the juice of 3
3 large eggs, separated, yolks lightly beaten
9oz fresh ricotta (if possible, not sterilized preserved stuff), drained in a sieve
1 cup all-purpose flour, sifted with 2 teaspoons baking powder
¼ cup ground almonds, freshly ground if possible
confectioners' sugar, to serve

Preheat the oven to 350°F. Butter an 8-inch springform cake pan.

Beat the butter and sugar together in an electric mixer until pale and fluffy, then beat in the
zest. Gradually add the egg yolks, beating well after each addition. Drain off any liquid that
is in the ricotta (there's usually a little). Stir the drained ricotta into the batter.

Beat the egg whites until they form medium peaks. Stir the lemon juice into the batter,
then fold in the flour, almonds, and baking powder. Fold two big spoons of the beaten egg
whites into the batter to loosen it, then fold in the rest. Scrape the batter into the prepared
pan. Put it in the oven and bake for 45 to 50 minutes. A skewer inserted into the middle
of the cake should come out clean once it's cooked. It is a very moist cake because of the
ricotta, and doesn't have the texture of a regular cake.

Carefully unlatch the sides of the springform pan from around the cake and let it cool.
This is lovely just slightly warm, but you can let it cool completely. Dust with confectioners'
sugar and serve with berries and crème fraîche or whipped cream.

raisin, lemon & marsala bread & butter pudding

BREAD AND BUTTER PUDDING—and limitless riffs on it—has been my "go-to" dessert for the last 20 years. This has a Sicilian spin. Make it twice and you won't have to think about it and can adapt it at will. The unchangeable elements are the quantities of milk, cream, eggs, sugar, butter, and bread. Put it in the oven as soon as your guests arrive.

SERVES 6

⅔ cup raisins

½ cup Marsala, plus more if needed

1¼ cups whole milk

1¼ cups heavy cream

2 broad strips of unwaxed lemon zest, plus finely grated zest of ½ lemon

¾ cup superfine sugar

pinch of salt

3 large eggs, plus 1 egg yolk

½ teaspoon vanilla extract

½ stick unsalted butter

about 9oz sweet bread, such as challah or brioche, sliced

confectioners' sugar, to dust

Put the raisins into a small saucepan and add the Marsala. Bring to just under a boil, then remove from the heat and let plump up for 30 minutes.

Bring the milk, cream, broad strips of zest, ½ cup of the sugar, and the salt to a boil in a heavy pan. Remove from the heat. Beat the eggs, egg yolk, and remaining sugar with a wooden spoon. Slowly pour the warm milk onto this, stirring all the time, then add the vanilla extract.

Butter the bread then layer it, buttered-side up, in an ovenproof dish, sprinkling on the finely grated zest, raisins, and Marsala as you go (if all the Marsala has been absorbed, sprinkle a little more on as you layer it). Pour the cream through a sieve onto the bread and let stand for 30 minutes (this will make the pudding lighter). Preheat the oven to 350°F.

Put the dish in a roasting pan and add enough boiling water to the pan to come halfway up the sides of the dish. Bake for 40 to 45 minutes, or until puffy, golden, and set on the top (if you press the middle with your finger it should be *just* set). Let cool slightly; the pudding will continue to cook a little. Dust with confectioners' sugar and serve with crème fraîche or whipped cream.

raspberry yogurt cake

I HAD A LOVELY yogurt and raspberry cake in a café, The Field Kitchen, in Nettlebed near Henley, in Oxfordshire, and could not get it out of my head. This is my version of the cake I couldn't forget. You do have to eat it on the day it's baked, otherwise the raspberries in the icing will spoil.

SERVES 10 TO 12

For the cake
1¼ sticks unsalted butter, plus more for the pan
1 cup superfine sugar
finely grated zest of 2 unwaxed lemons
½ teaspoon vanilla extract
2 large eggs, at room temperature, lightly beaten
2½ cups all-purpose flour, sifted
2 teaspoons baking powder

½ cup plain yogurt
1⅔ cups raspberries

For the icing
1½ cups sifted confectioners' sugar
2 tablespoons lemon juice
about 10 raspberries

Preheat the oven to 350°F. Butter an 8½ x 4½ x 2½in loaf pan and line the bottom with nonstick parchment paper. Beat the butter and sugar until pale and fluffy, then add the lemon zest and vanilla. Add the eggs a little at a time, beating well after each addition. Put 2 tablespoons of the flour in a bowl to toss with the raspberries later. Mix the remaining flour and baking powder together and fold this into the batter, alternating with spoonfuls of the yogurt.

Toss the raspberries with the reserved flour. Put one-third of the batter into the loaf pan and add half the raspberries, spreading them out evenly. Put another one-third of the batter on top, followed by the rest of the raspberries. Finish with the remaining batter.

Bake for one hour 15 minutes. A skewer inserted into the center of the cake should come out clean when the cake is ready. If the top seems to be coloring too much during cooking, cover it with foil. Let the cake cool in the pan for 10 minutes, then turn it out onto a wire rack and let stand until cold.

Mix the confectioners' sugar with the lemon juice until smooth. Spread about two-thirds of this on the cake. Partly crush the 10 raspberries and add them to the remaining icing. Don't completely mix them in; you just want them to stain some of the icing. Pour the raspberry and icing mixture over the cake. This won't set firmly, but do let it set a little before serving.

turkish mocha pots

MOST PUDDINGS IN TURKEY are fruit- or pastry-based, but I ate a spiced chocolate mousse when I was last there and decided to combine it with the flavors of a Turkish coffee. This is easy to make and there's no last-minute fiddling around. Make sure you cover the pots with plastic wrap, or they'll pick up other flavors while they're in the fridge.

SERVES 6

1 cup whole milk

1 cup heavy cream

ground seeds from 5 cardamom pods

½ cinnamon stick

¼ cup soft dark brown sugar

2 tablespoons cornstarch

1½ tablespoons instant espresso coffee

7oz high-quality dark chocolate (70% cocoa solids), broken into pieces

2 tablespoons unsalted butter

1 teaspoon vanilla extract

1 cup heavy whipping cream

2 tablespoons confectioners' sugar, or to taste

chocolate-coated coffee beans

Put the milk and cream into a saucepan with the cardamom and cinnamon. Bring to a boil, remove from the heat, and let sit for 30 minutes so the spices can flavor the milk. Strain.

Mix the sugar, cornstarch, and coffee together in a saucepan. Whisk in the milk mixture, adding it slowly so that no lumps form. Set over medium heat and bring to a boil, stirring constantly, then remove from the heat. Add the chocolate, butter, and vanilla and whisk until the mixture is completely smooth and the chocolate has melted. Divide among six little pots or coffee cups. Cover with plastic wrap and refrigerate for at least two hours to firm up.

Whip the cream, add the confectioners' sugar, and use it to decorate each pot or cup. Top off with two or three of the chocolate-coated coffee beans to serve.

shopping guide

There is hardly an ingredient that you can't find online these days, but I recognize that no one wants to have to make an online order—with the added delivery costs—every week. I've tried to give alternatives for ingredients that are not easy to find (though supermarkets stock an incredible range of ingredients these days), but there are a few you might need to track down. What I sometimes do is make a list of several ingredients and put in an order with a single company, to save money on delivery costs.

There are some grains used in this book that haven't quite made it into supermarkets yet (it's still hard to find farro, for instance, though you can substitute spelt) and also a few chile pastes. Here in the UK, my first stop is usually a company called Souschef. They're quick, reliable, and offer great customer service. American online suppliers are listed here, especially for unusual spices.

When it comes to fruit or vegetables that are more difficult to find, farmer's markets, ethnic supermarkets and family-run neighborhood grocery stores are often happy hunting grounds.

I don't order fish online; I don't often buy it in supermarkets, either. I usually go to my fish dealer. I have a really good local butcher, too, but I buy the occasional piece of meat from the supermarket. Never, however, pork. For that you do need a butcher and an excellent one at that. I don't like to be impractical or sound snobbish but, honestly, if my only option for pork chops is the supermarket, I prefer to just make something else instead. I also order some meat online, especially sausages, directly from the producer. Have a look around the internet or in some local directories. There may be other amazing farms and farm shops in your area just waiting to be discovered.

D'ARTAGNAN
www.dartagnan.com

This is an online supplier of conscientiously raised meat, including pork from Berkshire pigs, a heritage breed. D'Artagnan are committed to free-range, natural production and sustainable, humane farming practices, and partners exclusively with small farms and ranches that have strict standards, never use antibiotics or hormones, and sign affidavits to that effect. Order are packed in a refrigerated facility in insulated boxes with enough ice packs to keep the meat safely chilled for up to 48 hours in transit. All orders are shipped via FedEx for next day delivery.

LOS CHILEROS DE NUEVO MEXICO
www.loschileros.com

This online supplier offers a very wide variety of organic, all-natural chiles, in either whole or powdered form.

NUTSITE
www.nutsite.com

The comprehensive site of a nationwide supplier of an extensive range of nuts, dried fruit, seeds, beans, and rice.

SEASON WITH SPICE
www.seasonwithspice.com

First launched in Penang, Malaysia in 2011, this US-based company now supplies premium spices and handcrafted blends from countries across southeast Asia.

STARWEST BOTANICALS
www.starwest-botanicals.com

This online retailer supplies USDA-certified organic edible lavender flowers, in Extra, Select, and Super Grade. You can also order fruit teas, including peach, from them, as well as a vast selection of unusual herbs and spices.

VEDICA ORGANICS
www.vedicaorganics.com

Not just for "healthy" ingredients, but a particularly great source for pulses, whole grains, dried herbs, and spice mixes.

index

acknowledgments

Part of what I do is collect recipes, from home cooks, friends, and chefs. I did this before I started to write about food, and the exchange of dishes and ideas has been one of the great pleasures of my life. Roopa Gulati now has at least one recipe in every book I write (her food is just so good) and I thank her for the dishes in this volume (Mumbai toastie and Roopa's kheer with scented fruits). @foodwithmustard—who I met on Twitter and has become a friend—gave me the recipe for one of her family's favorite dishes, Ishita's masala chicken. Tim Bax is responsible for Tim's parmesan chicken; Sally Butcher, who owns the lovely Persian shop, Persepolis, in south London, allowed me to steal her Persian-inspired eggs; chef Ben Tish gave me the recipe for Roast cauliflower with Spanish flavors; the team at the American food website, Food52, served me the lovely apple, kohlrabi, and beet salad (Food52 team salad) when I met them in New York last year; and Naomi Duguid gave me her knock-out recipe for Burmese chicken.

Huge thanks to my former and current editors at *The Telegraph*—Elfreda Pownall and Amy Bryant—for their support, their sifting of ideas, their dedication to the cause, and being a pleasure to work with. My publisher, Denise Bates, continues to "get" it and creates an environment in which we can all do the best job possible. Also at Octopus I am grateful to Jonathan Christie, Katherine Hockley, and Sybella Stephens for guiding this project through from manuscript stage to book. Dear Kevin Hawkins and Caroline Brown, you're just the best in the business.

Finally, the team: my editor, Lucy Bannell, designer Miranda Harvey, photographer, Laura Edwards, and cooks Joss Herd and Rachel Wood. Thank you all for being inspiring, sparky, kind, fun, open-minded, patient, perfectionist, and always going the extra mile. I appreciate all the work you do. The joy of collaborating with you means I am always writing a book (as I would miss you all too much if I wasn't). Particular thanks to Lucy, to whom this book is dedicated, for editing my words for 14 years (first at *The Telegraph* and then at my publishers) with the utmost care, and for unfailing friendship and support.